The Daily Telegraph

NEW
PARTY
BOOK

by

EVELYN PAYNE

✸

A Daily Telegraph Book

FOREWORD

Here is a long-needed book whose purpose it is to improve party-giving. Evelyn Payne has been called "Britain's best-known party-giver" and the practical advice she offers in these pages is the outcome of years of catering for famous people.

She uses photographs and sketches to support her message that entertaining is at the heart of the home. She writes on the art in the Woman's Page of *The Daily Telegraph*.

Coming to London at a time of domestic crisis from a sheltered West Country life she took a shop in Knightsbridge and started a catering business without any previous knowledge of the trade. She was inspired by a deep love of home life and belief in entertaining as its outward expression. Now, with typical generosity, she wants others to benefit from her experience.

Perfectionist as well as party specialist, she shows us how much more attractive we can make our parties, dealing with christening and coming-of-age, a dance and wedding reception, as well as the small lunch or dinner party.

Evelyn Payne is destined to become an indispensable voice in thousands of homes. She can help us to make friends of our neighbours. She shines out when the numbers we intend to invite are bewilderingly large, tells us with authority how to use an outside caterer and what we can do for ourselves, even to the exact information on the quantities of food, drink, crockery, cutlery and so on for parties of various sizes.

Menus, the drinks, flower decorations and enchanting table colour schemes—all are dealt with and practical recipes given so that the hostess can tackle her entertaining with fresh ideas and enthusiasm.

EVELYN GARRETT,

Editor, Woman's Page
The Daily Telegraph

A Daily Telegraph book published by Pitkin Pictorials Ltd.

© The Daily Telegraph

CONTENTS

1: THE ESSENTIAL "KNOW-HOW"

Any woman with a talent for thoughtfulness can be a good hostess, even in these competitive days when the standard of home entertaining is rising steadily. A little imagination will allow her to transfer herself into her guests' shoes. Standing at the receiving end she can judge the impression her hospitality will create.

To do this thoroughly she will need to make a mental run-through, starting with the arrival of the first guest. From this will emerge a detailed and comprehensive plan which will be the secret of her success.

Best curtain-raiser

A warm welcome by a gay, unflustered hostess is the best curtain-raiser to any party. Most women carry in their hearts an image of themselves in this flattering rôle. The hostess-with-a-plan is much more likely to get star rating than one who is wildly hoping to muddle through. Good parties do not just happen. I am not saying that impulsive, spur-of-the-moment ones cannot be enjoyable—very often they are enormously successful—but it is not wise to lean heavily on your luck after one such party. *It might not happen a second time.*

There are, of course, those happy people who can manage a hundred for drinks at the drop of a hat. These need no help from me; but for the hospitably-minded who need "know-how" to translate warm-hearted intentions into enjoyable reality these ideas on party planning are offered.

The help available

Never, since the days when the grandiose way of life got cut down to size and the butler and cook departed, has there been so much help available for home entertaining. Party aids are innumerable and a wise woman will acquaint herself with them. Some firms will travel miles to erect splendid marquees with sprung dance floors and elegant chandeliers or merely to cover in and present for you, in baffling disguise, a small backyard.

In almost every county there are people who will hire out china, linen, glass, cutlery and tables, while personal columns in local newspapers carry

. . . and the butler and the cook departed . . .

many offers of help in the shape of part-time barmen, waitresses, washers-up and so on.

There are also flower-arrangers, dance bands, entertainers and mobile barbecues available; and if, for a special occasion, a party-off-the-peg suits your requirements and pocket, a firm of caterers will move in and undertake the complete job for you, from toastmaster to ash-trays and with supper for the local police thrown in.

Five Golden Rules

For the enterprising hostess who intends to tackle the job herself, however, here are some golden rules:

NEVER despise a bit of good help, paid or unpaid. Don't deceive yourself into thinking that you can get by without it if your party is, with family support, for over 30, or 12 if you are alone.

ALWAYS recognise your physical limitations. It is not wise to redecorate the hall three days before the party (some people do!) or to wait until the day to try out a new recipe for lobster soufflé.

MAKE a friend of your wine merchant. He will advise you, supply drinks on "sale or return" basis, lend glasses free of charge, deliver and collect.

TRY to impart to each party a luxury touch—a beautifully decorated buffet table, perhaps, or something which has little to do with money but everything to do with individuality.

MAKE up your mind what type of party it is to be and see that your guests know. If it is a cocktail party followed by a buffet supper, make it clear on the invitation. I have seen odd situations arise when some guests have been asked to stay on by whispered invitation while the rest have clearly been expected to leave. This is prevalent but discourteous. A curious perversity seems to come over the unwanted ones, and I have known previously-warned guests to act as "decoy ducks", bidding their hosts a loud "Good Night" and walking round the block in an effort to get the lingerers on their way. It is much better not to have such complications.

Useful to know

Hired china and cutlery varies in price, according to district, from 2s to 4s a dozen. All this equipment comes in bulky containers, so have it delivered in good time to unpack and hide these temporarily in some out-of-the-way spot.

A barman for a cocktail party will charge you anything between £1 10s and £2. Arrange his fee when you engage him. He will expect a gratuity in addition to this. About 10s should make him happy; worth it if he's good and you want to use him again. He may have a girl friend who will assist in the kitchen or hand round food. She will expect about 25s. If they work after 10.30 p.m. they will charge a little more.

If you have decided views against their drinking during the evening, tell them so. In that case, leave tea-making equipment handy and offer them a gin and tonic when the party is drawing to a close.

One person can dispense and serve drinks adequately for 25 guests. One girl can serve a buffet meal for 20 but she will need help in the kitchen for hot dishes and coffee.

A toastmaster at a fee of 3 to 5 gns will steer inexperienced hosts right

Make a friend of your wine merchant.

through the formalities of a large and sophisticated wedding reception, taking rose-petals, tea for great-grandmother and orange squash for child attendants in his stride!

Write down your plan

When you begin your imaginary survey of the party scene, have paper and pencil to hand. Make columns and head them with the important items: Food, Drink, Help, Equipment, Flowers, and so on. Have one for Miscellaneous as well.

Then start with that first guest. Is your "daily treasure" going to open the door for him? Then put her in your Help column. A tray of drinks is the next thing. If a barman is going to serve them, put him on your list as well. Then in your Drink column put down what the drinks will be. The trays and glasses will go under Equipment and the ice under Miscellaneous.

As your imagination takes you step by step through the party programme, your lists will become more and more comprehensive, until, as you approach the end of your tour, you will have built up a complete estimate of requirements. You can then go ahead with your ordering, ticking off each item as it is dealt with.

A thoughtful touch here will be to remember if any of your guests needs a little special treatment—for example, an iced fruit drink for a teetotal guest, or a separate platter for a vegetarian one.

How many can I invite?

A party with too much space is as dampening to the party spirit as an overcrowded one is exhausting. Thoughtful planning will eliminate both faults. The average family house with a dining-room, a sitting-room, small breakfast-room or loggia and the usual kitchen will comfortably accommodate 80 guests for a cocktail party, 60 for a buffet-type meal and 40 for a formal lunch party or dinner. For the latter, have your rooms cleared of furniture and seat your guests at small tables. A 3ft 6in round table will seat six guests. You might use a 6ft or a 9ft trestle table against the longest wall and place two or three small round ones in front. Seat guests on one side only of the trestle table with their backs to the wall and not to the company.

A firm of removal contractors will clear your furniture if you cannot manage it yourself, take it away on a van and bring it back the next day. They will give you an estimate for this service.

Invitations

The once-complicated formula of social etiquette has changed and been simplified. The leaving of visiting cards for instance (right-hand corners turned down, one of one's own, two of one's husband's and delivered personally, please) is now just a quaint custom, as is, alas, the sending of flowers to last evening's hostess.

> Mr & Mrs. G. Johnson.
>
> Mrs. Bertram Heighway.
>
> at Home
>
> June 21st.
>
> R.S.V.P.
>
> Dancing 10 p.m.   75, Ovington Place
>   S.W.3.

The invitation card, however, remains more or less traditional. An engraved card is still considered to be in good taste (how many times have you secretly run your finger over the lettering?) but there has been a certain amount of compromise. Except in the case of a coming-out ball or a large wedding many hostesses use an "open" engraved "at Home" card and fill in the blanks in their own handwriting. In this case the names of the invited guests are written in the top left hand corner, the hostess's name in the centre above the "at Home" and the date of the party immediately below. The hostess's address is written under the letters R.S.V.P. and the key to the type of party comes in the opposite corner where the words "Cocktails", "Buffet-Supper" or "Dancing" may be written in. The time is put in there also. Engraved "open" "at Home" cards cost about £2 10s a 100.

Engraved Cards

If you decide to have an engraved wedding invitation the plate for this will cost about 10gns which will be in addition to the cost of the cards—about £4 17s 6d a 100. Normally, once the invitations are printed, the plate becomes obsolete but a leading firm of London stationers have had the idea of making an ashtray out of the plate. This makes an attractive reminder of an important event.

The lettering on any printed invitation card should be very simple. Nothing ornate. Plain Roman capitals or copperplate are the best. For small informal lunch or dinner parties the invitation can be by letter.

2 : THE TRANSFORMATION SCENE

The party décor should fit its surroundings like a glove. The familiar characteristics should not be eliminated. A room with all furniture re- moved, the carpet up and an obviously hired waiter standing behind a trestle table-cum-bar does not add up to good hospitality. Rather, it places the undertaking on a purely functional level and induces guests to feel that they are being "got off the list".

If a room is to be used for dancing, of course a fairly thorough clearance is unavoidable. Even so, standard lamps, small tables and a chair or two could remain, tucked well up into corners.

Buffet table treatment

Avoid a white tablecloth. It tends to create an hotel atmosphere. A softly-draped covering in a shade which matches the existing colour scheme is better and enhances the personal atmosphere. Pastel-shaded drip-dry nylon, gathered on to a Rufflette tape, is both pretty and econo- mical for this. Felt in good strong colours gives a smart sophisticated effect. Box-pleated furnishing satin produces a lush look for a wedding reception or silver wedding celebration, while gingham or sateen can be used for a kitchen or barbecue-style party. Bouffant net makes a dainty, youthful im- pact for, perhaps, a girl's coming of age or engagement party.

With any kind of decoration, time must be taken into consideration: gathering, draping, pleating or flouncing cannot be achieved in a few min- utes. For goodness's sake get this job done the night before the party!

How to drape and swag a buffet table

Look at the sketches on page 11 and 12. First cover a trestle table com- pletely with a white tablecloth or sheet, allowing it to fall to the floor in front (Sketch 1). Box the corners and secure with drawing-pins and put a few more along the back edge of the table (Sketch 2).

Now start to drape with your chosen material. You can either gather this into a flounce or box-pleat it. If a gathered flounce is to be used allow enough material to give you adequate fullness. Stitch a Rufflette tape on to the material (Sketch 3), draw it up to fit the table and fix on to the edge

Sketch 1

Sketch 2

Sketch 3

Sketch 4

Sketch 5

of the table by attaching it to the under-cloth with large pins (Sketch 4). Care must be taken to avoid the pins showing. There is no need to drape the back edge of the table as this will be visible only to the helpers standing behind the buffet. It is better, however, to take the material a few inches round the back corners to give a neat finish. Sketch 8 (page 14) shows a draped and swagged table. For this effect a double layer of material is stitched to the Rufflette tape, fixed to the table as described, then the top layer is gathered up into swags and fixed with pins. Finish the swags with small posies of flowers or fruit and leaves (Sketch 5).

Alternatively, you can swag your table in the following way: place a double layer of material right sides down on top of the table, pin edges of material to the undercloth, parallel to the front edge of the table and then pull over and allow to fall to the floor. Now gather up the top layer into swags and fix with pins. Less material will be needed for this method as it is a more tailored draping.

Box-pleating

If the material is to be box-pleated, you will need for your fabric four times the length of the table. Place it right side down on to the top of the table, material edge to front table edge. Pin it firmly into pleats by pushing the pins right through the boxed lining close to the front edge of the table and with the pins lying parallel to the table edge (Sketch 6) then pull it over and allow to fall down to the floor, when the finished effect should be neat and tailored (Sketch 7).

If you wish, in all cases the top of the table may be covered in the fabric used for the draping. In this case, cut a piece of material a few inches wider and longer than the size of your table and pin securely to the boxed undercloth. Then proceed to drape as before.

For a *drinks party in the garden,* have the swags caught up with little bunches of cherries, leaves and borage flowers. A *teenage party* could have a table covering of checked gingham and posies of small peppers, radishes and lemons, with runner beans wired into loops (this is done by running florists' wire right through the beans and then bending them into shape).

An attractive idea is to have two differently-coloured materials, say pale lemon over peach, and make the posies of flowers of two colours.

A table in petticoats

If you have any small circular tables at which to seat guests, these look very attractive petticoated for special occasions. For a 2ft 6in circular table you will need 10yds of non-iron nylon or Terylene (pastel-coloured cotton is attractive, and being thicker needs less fullness, but it has to be ironed). Cut a yard from this 10yd piece to cover the table top. Stitch a heading along the remaining 9yds and thread a tape through it.

To dress the table, first cover it with an ordinary plain cloth or sheet which should be big enough to almost reach the floor. Now cover the top

Sketch 6

Sketch 7

Sketch 8

with the small piece which you have cut off and pin the surplus few inches to the underside of the table with drawing-pins.

Now take the taped flounce and drawing-pin one end of the tape firmly to the table edge and then, gathering the fullness evenly as you go, pin the flounce right round the table.

Trim the depth of the frill so that it just touches the floor. There is no need to hem the bottom. The frill can be stored ready for next time drawn up on a coathanger.

The bar

Full instructions for making this are given on page 28.

A terrace transformed

A party on the terrace on a warm summer evening. Could anything be nicer?

Try making a party room out of your terrace. Or use the part of the garden against the house. You will need a lean-to awning. It costs from £15 to have a temporary one measuring 24ft x 12ft fixed on to a terrace or wall. These are very gay and create a good party atmosphere. Your local marquee people will do this and will also fix canvas shields at either end in case the night air is chilly. You can easily take them down if they seem unnecessary.

For greater effect the terrace walls could be adorned with decorated garden trellis. You can buy this in widths and lengths to suit your purpose. It is quite easy to create a continental air with panels of this into which you have fastened trails of greenery with oranges, lemons and a bunch or two of grapes. Short pieces of pliable bamboo pushed into the oranges and lemons enable them to be fixed in place easily. Bunches of grapes can be tied on.

If you have small tables on the terrace you could petticoat them (see page 13 for instructions) in different shades of cheap silk or cotton sheeting.

The fruit bar

Trellis panels can also be used for a stall to use as a fruit-drinks bar. (See colour illustration facing page 33). Attach two panels of trellis to either end of a trestle table. They should measure 6ft from ground to top. Run supporting lathes across the top graduated in height to form the base for a sloping roof. Thatch the roof with wine bottle straws opened out flat; cover the front of the table with green material, or imitation grass, and decorate the whole thing lavishly with greenery and fruit.

If the weather is unkind

If you would like to have an "outdoor" party when the weather is against you, arrange it indoors but turn the party room inside out. That is, make the inside look like outside! Little 3-ply awnings painted in stripes can be fixed over the windows and the fireplace completely hidden by a bank of flowers. If there is a creeper growing on the outside wall round the window it might be possible to loosen the longest strands and bring them through the window attaching them to the inside walls.

In off-beat mood

One reason for wanting your party outside the house is if the off-beat mood is to prevail. In this case, if you are using a garage, barn or stable (even an attic or cellar), the walls may need a festive disguise.

A wall in disguise

If a wall is to be disguised, there are many materials available. Bunting, cotton sheeting, hessian or good crêpe paper can all be used. For instructions see page 100.

Another attractive way of decorating a garage or cellar is to paste sheets of white paper all round the walls. Large cut-outs are then fixed on, or they can be drawn on. Another alternative is the judicious use of panels of inexpensive scenic wallpaper.

3 : THE GARNISHING GAME

The garnishing game is a fascinating one. Once the habit is established, one sees possibilities in almost everything that grows in the garden. Today's hostess, with only limited domestic help at her disposal, has to learn how to make her impact with much less "song and dance" than her predecessors. One dish now takes the place of five or six courses. That dish, then, needs to be beautifully presented.

A keen interest in decorating, garnishing and presentation will quickly bring her culinary renown. It all depends on the approach. For instance:

A chicken in party style

A simple dish of cold chicken can be as safe as the Bank of England— but as dull as the City on a Bank Holiday. This is how you can make it exciting: Cube the meat of a cooked chicken, place it on an oval platter and dress it with good mayonnaise. Strew it over with green grapes, black olives and flaked almonds and surround it with a border of cooked rice soaked in orange juice, in the proportions of the juice of one orange to a pound of rice.

Frosted mint sprigs

There is no need to look very far for other garnishing ideas. Many are right there in the garden under our noses—a bed of mint outside the kitchen door makes a good start.

Small sprigs of mint can be dipped first into beaten egg-white and then into castor sugar. Spread the leaves out into shape and put to crystallise in the refrigerator on a sheet of paper. To use the sprigs: For a dinner party dot them here and there on a pyramid of lemon sorbet which has been piled up on to a silver dish (sketch 1, page 18) and delicately coloured and flavoured with a trickling of crème de menthe.

Use a sprig to garnish the centre of a carefully prepared grapefruit half. (Having removed the centre pith, cut sections in the usual way and insert alongside each section a slice of sugared mandarin orange).

Allow sprigs to set in the centre of strained mint jelly moulds for garnishing a dish of lamb (sketch 2).

Set tiny leaves of mint with a strawberry or cherry into ice cubes and use to decorate a summer wine cup. (See page 59)

Sketch 2

Sketch 1

More ways with flowers, fruit and vegetables

Use small border flowers—pinks, larkspur or single heads of antirrhinum, for example—with glossy bay leaves, to make a circlet to hold a small iced melon for a dinner party first course (sketch 3).

Sketch 3

To make an orange "cup" for a cold duck dish, take a half orange shell, scoop out any remaining pulp or pith, fill with balls of iced melon and stand on a "sunflower" of bay leaves (sketch 4).

Sketch 4

Use the blue of borage and one or two nasturtium blooms to show off a simple green salad.

Caramelise tiny onions, carrots and white turnips and arrange them round a meat roast.

Use incurved lettuce heart leaves as containers for individual fish and poultry salads, standing them on squares of crispbread for easy serving.

Turn out a savoury mousse from a straight-sided soufflé dish and press identical leaves of chicory upright all round it as you would the sponge fingers on a charlotte russe (sketch 5).

Sketch 5

THE GARNISHING GAME

Emphasise the fact that your cheese-board holds home-made wholemeal rolls by decorating with a small sheaf of ripe wheat.

Place a small tray full of young and colourful raw vegetables on a supper buffet table with bowls of good dressing conveniently near and encourage guests to make up their own salads.

Decorate a platter of smoked fish (trout and eel for the less wealthy, or add smoked sturgeon and smoked salmon if you feel rich) with trails of

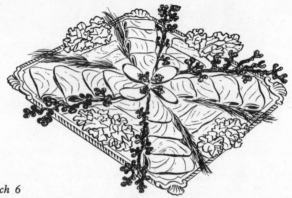

Sketch 6

seaweed, feathery fennel and large mussel shells filled with horseradish cream (sketch 6). "You chaps do yourselves pretty well," Prince Philip was heard to say when this first course was served to him at an all-male lunch.

Whenever I see rosy crab-apples, I want to make them into a posy to garnish a crown of lamb (sketch 7) which has been stuffed with pork and veal seasoned with rosemary and topped with a mould of crab apple jelly.

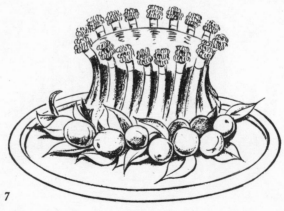

Sketch 7

20

Spiced plums and pears can be pierced at the top with small sprigs of lemon balm and used to garnish a dish of cold meats.

One or two small lemons, a white freesia bloom and a sprig of green leaves can be made into an effective spray (sketch 8) to decorate a cocktail tray of smoked salmon finger sandwiches. Florists' wire is useful here.

Sketch 8

Radishes or small tomatoes can be made into edible roses (sketch 9) by pressing level teaspoonsful of tinted, smooth cream cheese trimly against the sides in the shape of petals.

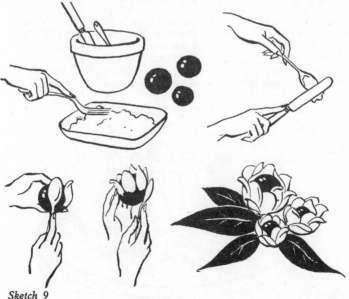

Sketch 9

21

THE GARNISHING GAME

A copious sprinkling of freshly-chopped parsley, mixed with chopped hard-boiled egg-whites and a little minced onion, will give a distinctly French look to many cold dishes such as brawn or sliced tongue. For easy cutting, put the egg-white into a cup or other container and stand in a pan of boiling water until it is firm. When cold, turn out and use as needed. This enables you to cut slices and shapes.

Lemon slices can be used in many ways. Cut a slice from the lemon and cut it across into two halves (sketch 10). Make a cut from the flesh edge inwards, stopping short at the rind (sketch 11). Holding the two ends of the half-slice with thumb and forefinger of each hand, twist it into an "S" shape (sketch 12).

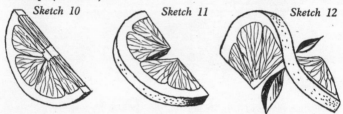

Sketch 10   *Sketch 11*   *Sketch 12*

To make a "butterfly" with the other half, make a cut, this time from the rind to the centre, but not quite through (sketch 13). Open it up into a butterfly shape and touch each "wing" with chopped parsley (sketch 14).

Sketch 13   *Sketch 14*

To make a flower-like edge to your lemon slices, cut narrow strips of peel lengthwise from the lemon, thus showing stripes of yellow and white (sketch 15). Slice the lemon across and the serrated edge will give the appearance of a flower (sketch 16). Touch with chopped parsley.

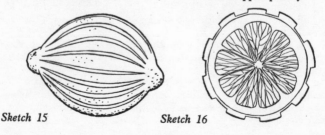

Sketch 15   *Sketch 16*

A "boat" which makes an attractive container for tartare sauce or mayonnaise is made from a lemon which is cut in half lengthwise, the pulp carefully removed and the edge serrated with scissors (sketch 17).

Sketch 17   *Sketch 18*

Tomatoes may also be made into "S" shapes, but this time use the whole slice (sketch 18). Or a slice may have a thin circle cut from the centre and be used as a holder for asparagus or little French beans. These vegetable bundles make a pretty garnish for a roast fillet of beef or veal.

Red or green peppers make a good natural garnish when sliced. The odd shapes are very decorative.

Small pineapples can be used with the green spiky leaves left on; cut one lengthwise through the middle and trim the flesh out. This makes two delightful "baskets" for fruit salad or strawberries. These can be finished off with a piping of whipped cream around the edge and laid together on a large silver tray to make a handsome contribution to a party table.

Melons can be used in similar fashion to pineapples.

A homely summer pudding looks wonderful if it is turned out on to a platter and surrounded by little clusters of fruits on small vine or raspberry leaves—red, black and white currants look particularly nice.

Arum lilies can be made from very thin slices of good-shaped white turnips. Shape into a cornucopia, insert a tiny strip of carrot as a stamen, secure the bottom with a small cocktail stick or toothpick and sprinkle a very little sieved, hard-boiled egg-yolk into the lily as pollen. These are lovely salad garnishes.

Minced radishes, alternating with chopped parsley, look very good when used on a rice border. They can also be used to colour cream cheese shapes on a cheeseboard.

The base of an artichoke, filled with Béarnaise sauce (see page 39) to garnish a tournedos steak, or filled with petits pois or asparagus tips to garnish chicken or lamb, gives a classic touch. These can be bought in tins and are invaluable.

Garnish for a whole salmon

Wrap the salmon in a folded cloth with the ends tied, to facilitate removal from the fish kettle when cooked. Put it into a fish kettle with warm water (to preserve the colour). Add seasoning and lemon juice. Bring to simmering point and never let it get beyond that. The water should barely move. For fish up to 5lbs in weight, cook for 7 mins to the pound, counting from the simmering point. For larger fish, allow 8 mins to the pound. Remove kettle from heat and allow the salmon to cool in the water.

You will need four strips of greaseproof paper or foil a few inches longer than the salmon, folded three or four times to a width of 8ins.

Place the salmon on one strip of paper. Remove the head and tail and take off the skin from the top half.

Run a sharp knife down the join which runs down the middle of the fish. Separate the two top halves from the under part of the fish

Put each half on a strip of paper. Remove the large spinal bone from the lower half of the fish. Also all small bones from the two top halves. You will find that there are about 14 long bones with heads in one of the top halves. Be careful to remove these; they look something like a darning needle. Remove all dark skin.

To remove the under skin of the salmon, turn the lower half over on to the fourth strip of paper. Remove the skin and fins. Holding the ends of the paper with both hands, turn the lower half, right side up, on to a serving platter. Replace the two top halves, leaving a gap in the centre about 2ins wide.

THE GARNISHING GAME

Brush the whole fish very liberally with aspic which is on the point of setting. Fill the centre space with prawns or shrimps. Garnish with radish roses, asparagus tips in rings of tomato, lettuce hearts and sliced cucumber.

4: THE COCKTAIL PARTY

Maltreated and maligned though it may be, this is still the most accommodating of parties. Its versatility is endless. Blown up into a gigantic jamboree it can inaugurate a motor-way, launch a deb or a battleship, introduce a diplomat or a smart new motor car or repay a year's hospitality. Whittled down to the "Come in for a drink" level, it still justifies its *raison d'être* in countless ways. There is scarcely one social event which it cannot adequately cover. Why, then, has it fallen into disrepute?

I think it is because this type of entertaining, so revolutionary in its informality and convenience when first adopted, was pushed too hard. Consequently, we got more and more overcrowded rooms, and ghastly experiments with food and drink—the feasts and the famines of the over-ambitious and the frugally-minded. There are now, thank goodness, welcome signs that these extreme practices have been played out and a much more enjoyable party is emerging.

... launch a deb or introduce a new motor car ...

Eight important points for success

Don't invite 200 guests when your room capacity is 80. They might all come!

DON'T limit your eats to nuts and olives on the assumption that "all my friends are dieting." This is an unkind practice; no-one should drink on an empty stomach, and it is guaranteed to drive away hungry, disgruntled and slightly tipsy guests in search of food.

DON'T on the other hand struggle to produce a bewildering variety of highly-coloured, highly-glazed and highly-messy so-called canapés. You need an army of efficient helpers to make good fresh ones.

DON'T use odd glasses from the back of the kitchen cupboard. The effect is untidy and unnecessary nowadays. Your wine merchant supplies them for nothing. A pink gin in an old mustard jar is a make-do which won't do.

Do offer guests immediately they arrive an easily-recognisable drink, with minerals, water or ice being added under their instructions. If it is a made-up "cup" or "bowle" *tell them exactly what is in it.*

Do delegate the serving of drinks if entertaining more than a handful of people. Concentrate on your duties as host, circulating and introducing people. It is still possible to keep a look-out for an empty glass and watch the state of supplies.

Do keep a reasonable room temperature. Doors should be removed if space is short, or opened wide. You should also open windows if necessary.

Do provide interesting and wholesome food. It is better to concentrate on four or five varieties which can be carefully prepared beforehand. Always bear in mind the fruit and vegetable dips for dieters and sandwiches for the conventional.

The bar

A small home can dispense with the bar and serve all drinks on trays from the kitchen or another suitable room. But if you decide you want one in the room, see that it is a good, workmanlike job with plenty of space behind for replacements of drinks and glasses. There should be a container handy to take away empties.

Place the bar at a focal point, away from the doors to avoid congestion; stand it in front of a window or fireplace, not forgetting that the "dispenser" must have easy access to the room where drinks are stored and glasses are being washed. A French window is perfect but a corner tends to take up too much room.

The ideal bar is made by a 6ft trestle table (30ins wide) standing 24ins away from the wall. This will serve 60 to 80 guests, a comfortable maximum for the average family house.

If you can't borrow or hire a trestle table any one of comparable shape will do. Cover the table with a large sheet or cloth, following boxing instructions (pages 11 and 13). If you want to make a feature of the bar, it could then be draped with some soft material in a pastel shade to match the room. Copy ideas from the buffet table décor (page 10).

A length of polythene across the top, which can have an occasional wipe over, will keep it spick and span throughout the evening. Keep this in place with drawing-pins. Don't clutter the table with flowers or candelabra.

The bar-box

Have ready a bar-box containing an ice-pick or strong skewer for breaking ice, tongs for serving it, crown openers, corkscrews, an optic measure for accurate and easy pouring, a bottle of bar syrup (see page 59), lemons, cocktail onions, Angostura bitters, cherries and small cube sugar.

Last minute reminders

Arrange for someone other than yourself to open the door, but be easily accessible to your arriving guests. Don't get trapped in a corner and find yourself unable to give a welcoming greeting.

See that all soft drinks and minerals are on ice for an hour before you start. Usually your fishmonger will supply ice, but give him a few days' notice.

Cigarettes are an optional offering but, if provided, there should be both tipped and untipped.

You will need ashtrays and book-matches galore in every possible place, and a "treasure" in the kitchen, washing glasses, equipped with a good supply of clean glass cloths. This is very important.

Things to note

If your kitchen is small and you have no other room available, it might be a good idea to have all the food refills which are not served hot put on to a small table outside the kitchen door.

The hot food should be laid out in deepish baking tins and put into a very low oven to be used as needed. Do not pile it up into double layers but keep everything flat, especially pastry.

The drinks

Spirits are a "must" at a cocktail party. A wine party is something completely different. One bottle of whisky or gin holds 27 fluid oz. A two-oz serving is a reasonable one, so you can estimate 13 drinks from one bottle.

Guests usually average three to four drinks in an evening, and the list given later is a useful guide. *The quantities are for 80 guests.* Order on "sale or return" so that you are not left with unwanted bottles.

A mixed tray is the best method of serving, even if the bar is in the room. If this is circulated it avoids congestion around the bar. It could hold, say, three glasses each of whisky and gin, two dry Martinis, one or two of sherry, a small bowl of ice with tongs to serve it, a syphon, three "splits" of tonic water, dry ginger and bitter lemon.

Your guests can then choose their own additions. This is very important as the lack of the right accompaniment can spoil the best drink.

Six to eight-oz stemmed goblets (known to the trade as Paris goblets) are the most suitable for these drinks. For shorter drinks, sherry or dry Martini, a five-oz goblet is more convenient in a crowded room than the usual sherry glass. There should also be a large jug of frosted fruit "cup" and some tomato juice.

What you need

The list given below is for the conventional type of cocktail party. (The quantities are on the lavish side for 80).

12 bottles Scotch whisky	*4doz "split" tonic waters*
12 bottles gin	*2doz "split" dry ginger ales*
2 bottles medium dry sherry	*3doz "split" bitter lemons*
2 bottles dry vermouth	*8pts fruit cup*
8 syphons soda water	*2doz small bottles of tomato juice*

Additional drinks

"Vodkatini" (vodka and dry vermouth)

Bacardi and lime (white rum)

A julep (Bourbon whisky with crushed fresh mint)

Brandy with ice, ginger ale or fresh orange juice (The wine snobs raise their eyes to the sky at this latter assortment — nevertheless these are very popular drinks).

A warning: I beg you not to offer your guests some unidentifiable drink economically concocted from the remnants of the drinks cupboard fortified by home-made parsnip wine and a drop of cider. It can make your guests ill and they can be justifiably suspicious.

The food

Remember the cocktail party is normally a pre-dinner party and not an evening meal. All the same, the trend is to provide more than just nuts and crisps.

Five varieties of savouries are ample, even if you have a few hungry guests, providing the party is finishing before 10 p.m.

One *pastry base*, one *sandwich base* (some guests always ask for "just a sandwich"), one *meat savoury*, one *fish savoury* and a *decorative dip* would lay the foundations for a balanced menu. These five varieties provide the key to your choice of food. Follow it and there will be something to please everyone.

The joy of this type of menu is that the hostess is not working like a beaver until the last moment. All hot food given here can be reheated successfully if it has been prepared in advance. Allow about two or three pieces of each variety per person and provide one dip for every 15 guests. Extra fillings for the dips could be ready and, as they begin to look a bit sorry for themselves, they could be whipped out into the kitchen, refilled and decorated.

A sample menu
(using one of each variety)

Miniature quiches Lorraine
Smoked trout and horseradish finger sandwiches
Stuffed prunes with bacon
Fish croquettes
Fruit and cheese dip

MINIATURE QUICHES LORRAINE
Cooked in small tartlet tins or could be cut in finger slices from one large one. (The first method looks neater, the second saves you time).

SMOKED TROUT AND HORSERADISH FINGER SANDWICHES
Made from thin buttered bread, one side white, one brown, cut length-wise from quartern loaves (you may have to order these). One loaf of each makes about 160 sandwiches. Fill with flaked, smoked trout, mixed with horseradish sauce, with a little extra cream added. Pepper well.

STUFFED PRUNES WITH BACON
The prunes are well soaked, stones removed and two cocktail onions inserted, then wrapped in thin streaky bacon and baked until bacon is crisp. These can be kept hot for some time without deteriorating.

FISH CROQUETTES
Finely chopped cooked and boned herring mixed with minced apple, chopped chives, parsley, and seasoning. Bound with beaten egg, rolled in crumbs and fried in deep fat. Serve hot on sticks.

FRUIT AND CHEESE DIP
Scooped-out melon and pineapple halves used as containers for a tangy cheese mixture can be laid out on one large platter made decorative with little mounds of celery curls, radish roses, baby carrots, apple slices, raw asparagus, melon balls on sticks (see page 35), pineapple cubes, chunks of cool cucumber and fingers of banana rolled in lemon juice and coconut. Use all these for dunking. (Baby spring onions if you dare!)

Other pastry bases
SWEETBREAD BOUCHEES
Bouchées of puff pastry cut with a 2in cutter, baked, and filled with a rich white sauce combined with well chopped sweetbreads, chicken, lobster or crab, mushroom or cheese.

CURRIED POPOVERS

Small squares of puff pastry given a filling of curried meat or poultry in the centre, corners turned to middle, brushed with beaten egg and baked. Serve hot.

ANCHOVY CRESCENTS

Cheese pastry cut into 2in circles, a strip of anchovy laid on, folded over to make crescents, brushed with beaten egg and sprinkled with chopped nuts. Bake until golden brown.

Other sandwich bases

Use several kinds of bread. Brown, white, crispbreads, pumpernickel, rye-bread and specially-made 2in rolls (coax your baker for the last).

Buy a 2lb sandwich loaf, called half-quartern. Cut this lengthwise (see page 106). Or order a 4lb quartern.

The slices can then be made into small open sandwiches, various-shaped double sandwiches, toasted sandwiches, or cut into strips 4in by 2in to roll round asparagus tips, bacon-wrapped fingers of sauté banana or tiny rolls of thinly-sliced rare cold beef wrapped around a half of a well-drained pickled walnut.

For roly-poly sandwiches (see page 89), use smoked salmon, minced ham mixed with French mustard, or savoury butter. These should be rolled up in greaseproof paper and put in the refrigerator for a few hours. They can then be sliced across like a Swiss roll.

The crispbread, pumpernickel and rye-bread can be used cut into various shapes and topped with button mushrooms, stalks removed, stuffed with crisp chopped bacon mixed with prune meat, tiny rolls of smoked ham wrapped round pieces of fig or banana, or a large slice of cucumber with a centre circle cut out and filled with flaked fresh salmon or shrimps or any colourful and piquant mixture.

In all cases before the toppings or fillings are added the bread should be spread with well-creamed butter. This prevents it from becoming soggy.

Other meat savoury bases

CHICKEN KIBBE

Small balls of minced, well-seasoned chicken with a little tarragon, bound with egg yolk, rolled in beaten egg and then in white crumbs and fried golden brown in deep fat. Put them on sticks.

SAVOURY CROQUETTES

Small croquettes of creamed potato mixed with cooked pounded chicken liver (well-seasoned), minced onion, a clove of crushed garlic and a sprinkling of thyme, bound together with beaten egg yolk. Roll in chopped almonds before frying in deep fat. Keep the temperature of the fat well below smoking heat and test by cooking one first. Put them on sticks.

KEBABS

Little squares of tenderloin of pork, a small slice of apple, a cocktail onion, a button mushroom and a tiny bacon roll, all previously cooked and then threaded on to a cocktail stick. Leaves of sage or bay can be added if liked.

BACON-WRAPPED CHIPOLATAS

Nothing new about these, but so popular that they can't be left out. Use very thinly sliced streaky bacon of a good quality to wrap around the small sausages. Ask your grocer to de-rind the bacon for you before slicing if you are using any quantity. Place each one close against the next in a baking tin (bacon join underneath) and cook beforehand for 30 minutes at Gas Reg. No. 4 (358 deg. F.) and re-heat when needed. Put on sticks.

Other fish savoury bases

STUFFED MUSSELS

Well-cleaned mussels, cooked in celery and onion-flavoured stock, taken from the half shell, a little cooked parsley and bacon stuffing inserted into the cavity where the beard was, and put back on to the shell with a cocktail stick through it for easy eating.

WHITEBAIT

There is no reason why these delicious little fish (below) may not be served to be eaten with the fingers. They should be lightly sprinkled with flour, fried in deep fat, well-drained and served on a large platter garnished with lemon. They should be dry and crisp. Season after cooking. Little rolls of thin brown bread and butter could also be used as a garnish. You will need a lot of these if you have many men at your party.

CRISPETTES OF SOLE

Small strips of sole, dipped into well-seasoned flour and fried golden brown. These must be crisp and well-drained. Serve on a platter with a bowl of tartare sauce for dipping them into.

TINY FISH BALLS

Any smoked or boiled fish well-seasoned, boned and pounded finely, can be mixed with half its weight of floury, mashed potato and two beaten eggs to a pound of fish. Shape into rounds and fry in very hot fat.

Other decorative dips

CUCUMBER AND YOGHOURT

Blend together in an electric mixer peeled cucumber cut into chunks (if no liquidiser, grate finely) and yoghourt to taste. This should be well seasoned with pepper and may need just a touch of green vegetable colouring and celery salt.

Serve home-made cheese straws in bundles, slotted through a ring of cheese pastry for dipping. Serve in a pottery bowl lined with incurving lettuce heart leaves.

PRAWN OR LOBSTER DIP

A large lobster or crab shell (below), makes an impressive container for the dip which can be a lobster bisque, thickened with stiffly-whipped cream or tartare sauce, or a mild aïoli (mayonnaise well-flavoured with crushed garlic). Cubes of lobster meat, scampi, or prawns are arranged on sticks and placed round the dip. Decorate it as well with a scooped-out lemon holding alternative sauce, and a few prawns still in their shells.

MINIATURE SWISS FONDUE

An ovenproof casserole with a small light beneath it is ideal for holding a bubbling piquant fondue. Buy the fondue tinned and dilute it with a little white wine. Use chunks of bread for dunking in it.

FRESH FRUIT DIP

Scoop out a large melon, fill with a mixture of honey, apricot juice, a little lemon to sharpen and a little cream cheese to thicken. Blend ingredients thoroughly in a mixer or whip up by hand.

Stand the melon on a platter decorated with vine or ivy leaves. Arrange around it little groups of fruits, melon balls shaped with a vegetable scoop and pierced with a cocktail stick, slices of apple dipped first in lemon juice and then in castor sugar, fingers of banana also dipped in lemon juice and then into grated coconut, small clusters of green and black grapes or cherries which are frosted in a similar fashion, small wedges of sugared pineapple and sections of frosted orange.

● ● ●

If you have found from experience that your parties are so successful that your guests won't go home at the proper time, don't be disconcerted. Be flattered but ready. A large hot dish such as Spanish paella could make its appearance any time after 9.30.

PAELLA (for 20 lingering guests)

This is a simplified version, without the traditional octopus. The average kitchen probably won't have a pan large enough to cook the quantities given all at once, so divide the ingredients. The first half may be cooked and kept hot until the second half is ready. In this case, all the chicken and shellfish may be added at the end. Serve with garnish of lemon sections and cooked mussels on the half shell.

INGREDIENTS: 6 tablespoonsful olive oil; 5 cloves garlic; 5 onions; 4 bay leaves; 6 cups Patna rice; 18 cups chicken stock; good pinch powdered saffron; salt and pepper; flesh from 2 large boiling fowls previously cooked in good stock (use this stock to cook the rice); mixed cooked shellfish (scampi, lobster, shrimps, mussels); 1 tin pimentoes (sweet peppers); 2 large packs frozen peas.

METHOD: Make the oil very hot in a heavy frying pan. Put in crushed garlic, chopped onions and bay leaves. Cook until onions are golden brown. Add the rice and turn over and over with a palette knife until it is soaked in the oil. Add half the stock and cook for a few minutes. Add saffron and seasoning, stirring to distribute colour. Add the remainder of the stock and cook for 20 mins. The stock should now all be absorbed and the rice cooked. Cut the pimentoes into strips and add together with the peas. Meanwhile remove the chicken flesh from the bones and cut into fairly large pieces. Add to the rice and cook a further few minutes. Finally add the shellfish.

5: SMALL DINNERS FOR
SPECIAL OCCASIONS

Good planning is never more valuable than for the small dinner-party. In the close, intimate atmosphere of the dinner table the hostess-cook must brave out her mistakes in full limelight, regretting the quiet hour she did *not* spend with pencil and paper.

Today's hostess has never before had such stimulating competition. Masculine interest and astonishing efficiency in the culinary field keep her on her toes. Men, nowadays, thoroughly understand the art of gracious living and what Brillat-Savarin called "the pleasures of the table."

Big business has taught many a young man interesting things other than the level of the bank rate or the state of the stock market. Home entertaining becomes as important to him as the luxurious lunches served in executive suites.

The feminine touch is still a trump card. A woman can impart elegance and imagination in a special way. Her table can be expressive of her personality, but only if she gives constant thought to it.

She should be always on the look-out for the attractive and unusual in table appointments. This is more a question of taste than money. Surely there is no harm in a hostess being a status-seeker where hospitality is concerned?

Here are some dinner-party plans. Each needs a candle-lit table and a cool, poised hostess.

The plan of action should be worked out three days in advance. All orders should then be placed. The day before, silver, linen, china and glass should be got out and the flowers done. If a petticoated table is to be used (see page 13) that should also be done.

If a plain cloth is to be used, a thick blanket or something similar should go underneath. This gives a much more luxurious look. Check on cigarettes. Check also on serving dishes, cooking pots and pans, and so on.

A SPRING DINNER-PARTY FOR SIX

Suggested table décor

Pale yellow cloth, mats or petticoat. Low arrangement of massed wall-flower heads of all shades.

The menu

Orange consommé en gelée	*Petits pois*
Poached trout with bananas	*Little new potatoes*
Filets mignons garnished with	*Fresh apricot cream*
fonds of artichoke filled with	*Coffee*
Béarnaise sauce	

The drinks

With the fish, the dry wine of Château Yquem, called Ygrec would be ideal but expensive. A light Moselle, or Macon such as Pouilly Fuissé, is more economical. With the meat, certainly serve a red Bordeaux according to taste.

Advance preparation

On the previous day or several hours in advance, prepare the consommé. Cook the apricots and leave to soak in the Kirsch. Assemble all dry ingredients necessary for cooking the dinner.

The recipes

ORANGE CONSOMMÉ EN GELÉE

INGREDIENTS: 2 large tins clear consommé; juice of 4 oranges; peel of 1 orange; 3 cloves; scant tablespoonful of aspic crystals.

METHOD: Remove the pith from the orange peel then cut it into thin strips. Put into boiling water for a minute or two. Put the consommé, orange juice, cloves and melted aspic crystals into a saucepan, then bring to the boil. Strain the orange strips and add. Put liquid into the refrigerator until needed. It should be only just set, not solid. Serve in soup cups with slices of orange as garnish.

POACHED TROUT WITH BANANAS

INGREDIENTS: 6 trout; 4 bananas; 4 shallots; 4 tomatoes; salt; pepper; tablespoonful tarragon vinegar; ⅓ bottle dry white wine; 1oz butter; 2 tablespoonsful of thick cream (not whipped).

METHOD: Wash and clean the trout. Place them in a fireproof dish. Slice the shallots and tomatoes and put them round the trout. Slice one banana and add that. Season well. Add wine and vinegar. Cover with foil and cook at Gas Reg. No. 4 (358 deg. F.) for 30 mins. While the trout are cooking slice the remaining bananas lengthwise into two halves and then across. Fry these lightly in the butter. Keep hot. When trout are cooked, take them out and carefully remove the top skin. Keep the heads on. Boil the cooking liquid very hard for about 10 mins to reduce it. Strain, then rub the residue through the sieve into the strained liquid. This makes the sauce.

Stir this sauce well, correct the seasoning and stir in the cream. Spoon a little of this over each trout, then put under the grill for a minute or so. Place two pieces of the fried banana on each fish and serve.

FILETS MIGNONS GARNISHED WITH ARTICHOKE FONDS FILLED WITH BEARNAISE SAUCE

INGREDIENTS: 6 slices of fillet of beef, cut from the small end of the fillet (about 4oz each); olive oil; 6 artichoke fonds (it is easier to buy these tinned); Béarnaise sauce; watercress for garnish.

First make the sauce:

INGREDIENTS BEARNAISE SAUCE: 4 shallots; 2 tablespoonsful wine vinegar; 4 tablespoonsful dry white wine; 1 teaspoonful chopped tarragon (dried will do); pinch chervil; 4 egg-yolks; 2oz butter; salt; pepper.

METHOD: Chop the shallots and put into a saucepan with the vinegar, wine, some of the tarragon and chervil. Bring to the boil and let the liqui reduce by two-thirds. Let it cool. Add the egg-yolks and stir well. W stand the saucepan in hot water and add a drop of cold water. Then add, a little at a time and stirring throughout, the butter cut into small pieces. Season with salt and pepper. The sauce should now be as thick as cream. Strain and add a little more chopped tarragon.

Keep the sauce warm while you season and grill the steaks. When ready to serve, warm the artichoke fonds in a little of the liquid from the tin, fill each one with Béarnaise sauce and put one on each fillet. Garnish the dish with watercress and hand extra sauce.

PETITS POIS

Use fresh peas or two 10oz packets of frozen peas. Put into a saucepan with a little butter, sugar, salt, one or two lettuce leaves and a few spring onion bulbs. Fresh peas will need a little water. Cook gently on a low heat for 30 to 40 mins. Strain off most of the liquid and remove lettuce before serving. It is not necessary to thaw the peas before putting them into the pan.

NEW POTATOES

You will need about 1½lbs of new potatoes. Boil, strain and toss in hot butter and chopped parsley.

FRESH APRICOT CREAM

INGREDIENTS: 1lb fresh apricots; about ½lb castor sugar; ½pt double cream; miniature bottle Kirsch.

METHOD: Poach the apricots in water to cover with about half the sugar. (Taste to see if more sugar is necessary). Remove from the syrup, stone and cut up roughly. Pour on the Kirsch and leave to marinate for about an hour. This can be done the night before if liked. Remove apricots from the marinade and reserve liquid. One hour before ready to serve whip the cream until it gets thick and light but not "curdy." Stir in the rest of the sugar. Fold the cream lightly into the apricots, add a little of the Kirsch marinade and chill until ready to serve. Serve in individual dishes.

A JUNE DINNER-PARTY FOR SIX

Suggested table décor

Use a white lace tablecloth, petticoat, or white lace mats. Have white candles on the table as well. Arrange a centrepiece of red roses and place single blooms at the candle bases. For melon wreaths see page 18.

The menu

Curried melon
Butter stuffed mushrooms
Baby lamb

Platter of young vegetables
Fresh strawberries Romanoff
Coffee

The drinks

Nothing but water should ever be drunk with curry. With the lamb, choose a red wine of Beaujolais or Macon—preferably a 1959 and certainly not older than 1957.

Advance preparation

On the previous day or several hours in advance, prepare melons and put into the refrigerator. Get mushrooms ready for dipping into the batter. If using garden vegetables with the lamb the preparation should be left until as late as possible but if they are shop-bought you might as well get them done in advance. Assemble all dry ingredients.

The recipes

CURRIED MELON

INGREDIENTS: 6 Charentais melons or 3 small Honeydew or Canteloupe; ½pt stiff mayonnaise; ½pt double cream; curry sauce.

INGREDIENTS FOR THE CURRY SAUCE: 1 large onion; 1 apple; 1oz butter; 1 tablespoonful honey; 2 tablespoonsful curry powder; 1 tablespoonful tomato purée; glass of dry white wine; small glass of water; salt; pepper; 2 tablespoonsful apricot jam or purée.

METHOD FOR CURRY SAUCE: First make the curry. Chop the onion and apple and put into a sauté pan with the butter. Cook for a few minutes then add the honey, curry powder, tomato purée, wine, water and a little salt and pepper. Simmer very gently together for 30 mins. Allow to cool. Rub through a sieve, also sieve the apricot jam or purée and add that to the curry mixture. Allow to cool.

Fold this mixture in to the mayonnaise.* Lastly whip the cream until it is thick but not "curdy". Fold it into the curried mayonnaise.

TO PREPARE THE MELONS: Charentais melons are served one to each guest. The Honeydew or Canteloupe are served in halves. To serve Charentais melons a slice is cut from the top and the seeds removed. The flesh is scooped out into small balls with a vegetable cutter. The Honeydew or Canteloupe melons are first cut in half. Cut a thin sliver from the bases to make them stand firmly. The melon balls are thickly coated with the curry sauce and returned to the skins. Chill well before serving. Garnish with flowers (see page 18).

*THE MAYONNAISE

INGREDIENTS: 2 egg-yolks; ½pt olive oil; good pinch of salt and pepper; 1 or 2 teaspoonsful of vinegar.

METHOD: Beat the egg-yolks and salt with a wire whisk for 10 mins. They will thicken. Add a drop or two of vinegar to make them almost liquid again and beat once more. Add a drop of oil, beating well. Continue dropping the oil, a very little at a time, until you see that the mixture has "taken." Always beat in the same direction. When the mixture becomes too thick, add a few more drops of vinegar. You can now begin to be more liberal with the oil but beat well all the time. Add pepper and more salt if necessary. Continue until all the oil is absorbed. This makes a thick mayonnaise and can be made lighter by the addition of whipped cream or whatever your recipe calls for.

BUTTER STUFFED MUSHROOMS

INGREDIENTS: 18 large mushrooms; 1lb butter; batter; oil for deep frying.

METHOD: Remove the mushroom stalks. Peel the caps and sauté them in a little butter. Allow to become quite cold. Melt the rest of the butter and dip the caps into it, holding each one underside uppermost so that the hollow part is filled with the liquid butter. Place carefully on a tray and put into the refrigerator until the butter is set very hard. Have ready the batter* and hot fat. Dip each mushroom cap into the batter. Fry in the deep fat. Drain and serve with tartare sauce and wedges of lemon.

*THE BATTER

INGREDIENTS: 8oz plain flour; 1 tablespoonful baking powder; salt; 1 cup of lukewarm water; 2 tablespoonsful of vinegar.

METHOD: Mix the flour to a thick paste with the warm water. Add the baking powder. Season. Add the vinegar and mix well.

This batter will stay crisp for a long time and will re-heat quite satisfactorily.

BABY LAMB WITH YOUNG VEGETABLES

INGREDIENTS: Small leg of lamb; 12 small onions; 12 tiny, new potatoes; 6 new carrots; 6 small, new turnips (white); 1lb shelled peas; 1lb French beans; 2 cloves garlic; sprig of rosemary; ½pt water; ¼lb butter; salt and pepper.

METHOD: Prepare the vegetables and put them into a roasting-pan. Season, add the crushed garlic and rosemary. Add water and butter. Take the grid from your grill-pan and put it into the roasting-pan, arranging the vegetables underneath it so that they do not become crushed. Rub the lamb with salt and pepper and place it on the grid. Bring the liquid in the pan to the boil on top of the stove. Cover with foil and put into the oven at Gas Reg. No. 4 (358 deg. F.) Cook for about 2 hours. Baste frequently with the liquid in the pan. To serve, remove the rosemary, put the leg on a platter with little mounds of the vegetables round it. Try to keep them separate—a group of potatoes, one of carrots, one of onions and so on.

Skim the fat then serve the juice from the pan separately.

FRESH STRAWBERRIES ROMANOFF

INGREDIENTS: 2lbs fresh strawberries; castor sugar; miniature bottle of Cointreau; juice of 2 oranges; cream.

METHOD: Hull the strawberries. Sprinkle liberally with sugar. Pour over the strained orange juice, and add the Cointreau. Chill until ready to serve with cream.

HIGH SUMMER DINNER-PARTY FOR SIX

Suggested table décor

Pale green cloth, mats or petticoat. Floating water lilies or white peony heads. Water lilies will close up at night, so weight down each petal where it joins the stem with a drop of melted candle fat.

The menu

Iced cucumber soup
Timbales of fresh spinach and mushrooms
Escalopes of veal à la crème

Braised courgettes (baby marrows)
Sorbet of fresh raspberries
Coffee

The drinks

If you can get it, the very light wine from Cordoba, Montilla, after which the Amontillado sherries are named, would go very well with the iced soup. Veal usually calls for claret, but for variety a Tavel rosé would blend very well.

Advance preparation

On the previous day or several hours in advance, make cucumber soup. Prepare the raspberry syrup for the sorbet. Assemble all dry ingredients. When actually cooking the dinner, have a large bowl of hot water and wash and put away everything as you finish with it. This only takes a few minutes and you will get on much more quickly with a tidy kitchen.

If you have no help at all during the dinner, do as a butler would do and have a small serving table just outside the dining-room door. A tea-trolley is splendid. Have a 7lb stone jam jar full of warm soapy water underneath and pop the used cutlery into it as you bring it out. Soiled plates go underneath, the top shelf holds the warmed plates. Delegate the serving of the wine.

The recipes

ICED CUCUMBER SOUP

INGREDIENTS: 2 large cucumbers; 2 small onions or shallots; 1pt milk; 1pt water; ½oz arrowroot; ⅓pt cream; seasoning; little green colouring.

METHOD: Peel the cucumbers, cut into pieces and add with the chopped onions or shallots to the milk and water. Cook together gently until cucumber is tender. Rub through a sieve. Add a little of the cream to the arrowroot and mix to a smooth paste. Stir this into the soup and cook for a minute or two until it thickens. Season. Stir in the rest of the cream. Colour a very pale green with vegetable colouring. Stand in the refrigerator until ready to serve. Sprinkle with a very little chopped chive.

TIMBALES OF FRESH SPINACH AND MUSHROOMS

INGREDIENTS: 2lbs fresh spinach; ½lb mushrooms; 2 eggs and 1 extra yolk; plenty of seasoning; 1 tablespoonful of double cream; a little butter.

METHOD: Wash the spinach well and cook with very little water and plenty of salt. Drain thoroughly and chop coarsely. Beat the eggs and extra yolk and mix into the spinach. Add pepper. Meanwhile, sauté the peeled mushrooms in the butter and slice them. Add the cream to the spinach. Butter six small moulds. Put in a layer of the spinach then a layer of mushrooms. Cover with another layer of spinach. Stand the moulds in a baking pan holding a little water. Cover with greased paper. Bake at Gas Reg. No. 4 (358 deg. F.) for ¾ hour. To serve, turn out on to a platter. If liked pour over a little warmed cream with sliced sautéd mushrooms added.

ESCALOPES OF VEAL A LA CREME

INGREDIENTS: 6 thin slices of veal; small glass of brandy; ¼lb butter; flour; salt; pepper; 1 cup of double cream.

METHOD: Flour and season the veal slices. Melt the butter in a sauté pan (it is essential to use a heavy, thick-bottomed type) and brown the veal very lightly on both sides. Reduce the heat and cook gently for 15 mins. Heat the brandy, take the veal from the sauté pan, put it on to another dish, pour over the hot brandy and light it. Let it blaze until the brandy has burned away. Add the cream to the pan, stir well to mix in the meat juices, return the veal to it and let it simmer for a few minutes. Correct the seasoning and serve. Garnish with lemon slices, olives and anchovies.

BRAISED COURGETTES

INGREDIENTS: 1½lbs to 2lbs very small courgettes; butter; salt; pepper; 1 crushed clove of garlic; chopped parsley.

METHOD: If very small, leave the courgettes whole. Do not peel them. Cook until tender very gently in butter and a drop of water to which garlic and seasoning have been added. To serve, add a little more butter and sprinkle with chopped parsley.

SORBET OF FRESH RASPBERRIES

The making of sorbets and ices at home is a complicated business and not to be recommended to the busy cook-hostess. There are excellent ready-made ones available. I suggest for this menu that a ready-made one is used as a base.

INGREDIENTS: 1½pts lemon or raspberry sorbet; 1lb fresh raspberries; castor sugar; miniature orange Curaçao; sprigs of mint for garnishing.

METHOD: Reserve the best of the raspberries for garnishing and cook the rest with sugar and a very little water. Cook slowly and with sufficient sugar to make a syrup. When ready strain and allow to become very cold. Pile the sorbet on a dish, pour over the orange Curaçao, then the syrup. Dot the pyramid with the rest of the fruit and little sprigs of mint.

A large daisy-sprigged pineapple would make an attractive container for this. Cut the top from the pineapple and scoop out the inside. Trim the base to make it stand firmly. Cover the entire surface with white daisy or marguerite heads wired through the centre with hair-pins or U-shaped pieces of florists' wire. Pack in the sorbet and replace the pineapple foliage.

AN AUTUMN DINNER-PARTY FOR SIX

Suggested table décor

Dark brown lace or linen cloth or mats. Have a centre arrangement of gilded cobs of corn. Use four or five cobs, turn back the transparent outer leaves and shape like petals. Spray with gold paint (aerosol sprays are available at most hardware stores), and arrange points uppermost in dampened plastic foam in a shallow container. Add a few small sprays of gilded beech leaves and half a dozen large horsechestnuts.

The menu

Smoked fish platter   *Dauphinoise potatoes*
Casserole of grouse   *Profiteroles in chocolate sauce*

The drinks

The smoked fish calls for white Burgundy or even Hermitage rather than Bordeaux. One of the fine vintages of Meursault would be ideal if you care to pay the price. With the grouse, go for a red Burgundy of the Côtes de Nuits. The chocolate sweet would naturally go well with Sauternes of some sort.

Advance preparation

Two days before, marinate the grouse. Previous day cook the casserole but do not thicken the sauce until an hour or so before serving.

The recipes

SMOKED FISH PLATTER

INGREDIENTS: 3 smoked trout; 6 slices smoked salmon; 6 1in pieces smoked eel; 6 slices smoked sturgeon if available (this chicken-like delicacy is not easy to obtain, but can be bought in Soho and at a few good delicatessen shops); horseradish cream; lemon sections.

METHOD: TROUT. Skin the trout and remove the heads. Split in two and remove the backbones. Cut each half in two pieces. SMOKED SALMON. Fold the slices over, keeping shapes as identical as possible. SMOKED EEL. Remove the skin. SMOKED STURGEON. Neat slices.

To arrange your platter: To make an attractive pattern, see illustration on page 20. Fill six large mussel shells with horseradish cream and dot between the layers of fish. If possible, garnish with long fronds of seaweed, otherwise use light-coloured leaves of celery. Finish with thick riders of lemon. (See page 22). Hand small rolls of thin brown bread and butter (see page 114) and extra lemon sections.

CASSEROLE OF GROUSE

INGREDIENTS: 4 old grouse (old grouse nicely cooked more than equal in flavour expensive young birds. This recipe justifies time and trouble);

marinade liquid*; 3oz butter; ½pt stock; glass red wine; bouquet garni (thyme, bay and parsley); seasoning; 2 tablespoonsful redcurrant jelly; 12 button onions; 12 button mushrooms; ¾oz flour; glass of Scotch whisky.

*THE MARINADE

INGREDIENTS FOR MARINADE: 1 large onion; 2 shallots; large glass red wine; 2 bay leaves; sprig fresh thyme or pinch of powdered; 2 tablespoonsful olive oil; teaspoonful bruised black peppercorns; coffeespoonful salt.

METHOD FOR MARINADE: Slice onion and shallots and mix all ingredients together. Split the birds in half, cut off the drumsticks and wings (these may be cooked in the casserole with the breasts for flavour but are not worth serving) then cut each breast in half with kitchen scissors. Stand the pieces in the marinade for 24 hours, turning several times.

METHOD FOR CASSEROLE: Remove joints from the marinade and wipe dry. Heat 2oz of the butter in a heavy pan. Put in the joints and cook for a few minutes. Take out and put into a deep casserole dish. Strain over the marinade liquid. Add the stock, red wine, bouquet garni, seasoning and redcurrant jelly. There should be enough liquid to cover the joints. Cover tightly and cook in the oven at Gas Reg. No. 3 (336 deg. F.) for 2 hours. Add the onions and mushrooms and cook for approximately another hour but test for tenderness and adjust time accordingly. When cooked, remove the bouquet garni and strain off the liquid. Blend the flour with the remaining ounce of butter, stir into the liquid, bring to the boil and cook for a few minutes. Add the whisky, stir well. When smooth, pour over the grouse, arranging the onions and mushrooms on top. Garnish with crescents of puff pastry or fried bread, bacon rolls and watercress. Hand redcurrant jelly.

DAUPHINOISE POTATOES

INGREDIENTS: 2lbs potatoes; 1pt milk or milk and cream; 1 egg; 1oz butter; ½ clove garlic; salt and pepper.

METHOD: Slice potatoes into very thin rounds. (A piece of French equipment, a mandoline, does this job very efficiently). Rinse and dry well. Butter an ovenproof dish and fill with layers of potato slices, seasoning as you go. Beat the egg into the milk, add the crushed garlic and a little more seasoning. Pour over the potatoes and dot with the remainder of the butter. Bake in the oven at Gas Reg. No. 4 (358 deg. F.) for 1 hour. Brown under grill if necessary.

PROFITEROLES IN CHOCOLATE SAUCE

INGREDIENTS: 12 chocolate-iced and fresh cream-filled profiteroles or miniature éclairs; 1pt chocolate sauce*; ½pt double cream, whipped; 2 oz bar plain chocolate.

METHOD: Place the profiteroles in a serving dish then pour over the chocolate sauce. Pipe a decoration on top of this with the whipped cream and finish with curls of chocolate. To make these, warm the bar of chocolate slightly and grate on a coarse grater.

*CHOCOLATE SAUCE

INGREDIENTS: 4oz plain chocolate; 4oz castor sugar; 2 egg-yolks; ½pt thin cream; small glass brandy.

METHOD: In a bowl standing over boiling water, melt the chocolate and sugar. Stir in the egg-yolks and add the cream gradually. Keep over low heat for about half an hour, stirring frequently. Lastly add the brandy. Allow to cool and then pour over the profiteroles. Serve very cold.

A WINTER DINNER-PARTY FOR SIX

Suggested table décor

Cloth or mats of any strong colour to match the existing decorations. Centre table arrangement of gilded fruits.

To make this, pack a fruit stand with well-dampened plastic foam. Press a small cheap pineapple into the centre of it and arrange pears, apples, bananas, tangerines and camellia or ivy leaves round it. Fix one or two bunches of grapes into position with strong hairpins.

Tie a piece of paper round the green top of the pineapple and spray the whole arrangement with aerosol gold paint.

Remove the protective wrapping from the pineapple. This arrangement will keep for several weeks. It may sound extravagant but in the long run is much cheaper than using fresh flowers at this time of year.

The menu

Melon and avocado pear cocktail	*Creamed potatoes*
Roast young goose	*Orange surprise*
Red cabbage	

The drinks

Muscadet or any other wine of the Lower Loire should suit the acidity of French dressing on the melon and avocado pear cocktail. The goose might go well with a claret from the right bank of the river Gironde—a St. Emilion, perhaps (rather than a Médoc or red Graves). Orange surprise—perhaps with one of the sweeter "late gathered" hocks which bear the general description "spätlese".

Advance preparation

The day before or several hours previously, prepare the cocktail, stuff the goose, remove flesh from oranges and leave skins standing in cold water. Arrange and gild the fruits for the decoration.

The recipes

MELON AND AVOCADO PEAR COCKTAIL

INGREDIENTS: 1 ripe melon; 2 large avocado pears, 3 if small; teaspoonful chopped chives; $\frac{1}{2}$ small cucumber or $\frac{1}{2}$ cup chopped celery; 4 tomatoes, skinned and cut into sections; lettuce heart leaves; French dressing.

METHOD: Cut the melon in half and with a small vegetable scoop make as many small balls of the flesh as possible. Peel the avocados, take out the stones and dice the flesh. Add the chives, cucumber or celery and tomatoes. Dress with French dressing and chill. To serve, place incurved lettuce heart leaves in six stemmed goblets, champagne glasses or attractive individual glass containers. Spoon in the cocktail, topping each one with two or three of the melon balls. Serve very cold.

ROAST YOUNG GOOSE

INGREDIENTS: 1 young goose (8 to 10lbs); salt; pepper; 6 eating apples, peeled and quartered; 18 large prunes, soaked and stoned; apple chutney; 10z butter; 1 tablespoonful flour; cup of water; watercress.

METHOD: Rub the bird inside and out with salt and pepper. Stuff with the apples and the prunes which have been filled with a little apple chutney. Put into a roasting pan with the butter, then roast for 3 to $3\frac{1}{2}$ hours at Gas Reg. No. 4 (358 deg. F.) basting frequently. When almost done, baste with two or three tablespoonsful of cold water and leave the oven door open to crisp the skin. If you like a gravy with your bird, skim the fat from the liquid in the roasting pan, mix flour and water and add. Bring to the boil. Stir well, season and strain. For easy serving, carve the goose while guests are drinking their apéritif, cover with foil and keep hot. Before serving, garnish with the fruit stuffing and watercress. Hand the gravy.

RED CABBAGE

INGREDIENTS: 1 medium-sized red cabbage, shredded; 2oz butter; 2oz brown sugar; 2 large apples, peeled and sliced; 1 large onion, chopped finely; juice of 1 lemon; 3 tablespoonsful wine vinegar; salt.

METHOD: Melt butter in a thick saucepan, add the cabbage and sugar and cook over low heat for half an hour. Add remaining ingredients and cook very slowly for a further $1\frac{1}{2}$ hours. Stir frequently.

ORANGE SURPRISE

INGREDIENTS: 6 oranges; 6 portions of orange water-ice (buy ready-made or if unobtainable use vanilla ice-cream with a little orange juice strained over it); 2 egg-whites; 4oz castor sugar; few cubes of ice.

METHOD: Cut the tops from the oranges. Scoop out the flesh with a teaspoon. Make a stiff meringue with the egg-whites and sugar and fill the oranges with the water-ice or ice-cream. Cover top closely with the meringue, completely sealing in the ice-cream. Place in a baking tin with the ice cubes around and put into the top of a very hot oven Gas Reg. No. 7 (424 deg. F.) for two or three minutes or until meringue is nicely coloured. Serve immediately on a platter garnished with glossy green leaves and one or two white flower heads—freesia is attractive.

6: SUNDAY MORNING ON TWO LEVELS

Sausage, cheese and beer party for peasants (1)

The Sunday morning party, with many people, takes the form of a casual standing invitation to their friends: "We are always at home on Sunday after about midday."

This involves seeing that there is something in the house to meet the requirements of a number of people which may vary from half a dozen to 20 or so. Since many people no longer eat large breakfasts, that "something" must be reasonably substantial—what North Country folk call a "putting-on."

At the same time it is important to spare the housewife, since Sunday morning, the freest time of the week, must not be too much of a labour for her. So the first rule is to make it a relaxed party—if possible in the garden—with beer and a snack. Have a "pin" of beer and iced lager (see page 98). Nothing goes so well with beer as sausages and cheese, and nothing is less trouble. Large platters holding a variety of six or so English and continental sausages and a mixture of cheeses expertly laid out look very appetising.

At all sausage and beer parties serve . . .

Little chunks of hot French bread.

Large bowls of various mustards (dot these about, flagging them to show which is which). There should be English and French, both mild and strong.

FOOD FOR A MONTH OF WORK-FREE SUNDAYS

First Sunday: Mixed Sausage Platter

Continental tongue sausage　　*English liver sausage (cut thickly)*
Danish salami　　*Cumberland sausage (fried and*
Smoked ham sausage　　*cut into 1½in slices)*
Garlic sausage (Polish and so on)　　*Pickled cucumbers*

For each guest allow four oz of mixed sausage and salami. Bowls of watercress make a good addition.

Down the centre of your platter arrange a line of overlapping tongue sausage. On either side, a layer of salami lilies. Next to these comes a line of Cumberland sausage slices on sticks; then identical rows of liver sausage. Outline the edges of your platter with half circles of smoked ham sausage and garlic sausage. Intersperse with fans of pickled cucumber or gherkins.

SALAMI LILIES

To make a lily-shape from a slice of salami, cut from the outer edge to the centre. Overlap the cut edges until you have a cone shape. Fasten the cut edges together with a smear of butter. Place a cocktail onion in the centre of each cone.

CUCUMBER FANS

Cut pickled cucumbers or gherkins lengthwise in thin slices to within ½in of the end (less if you are using the small gherkin) and fan out like a hand of cards.

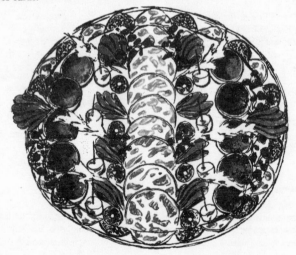

Second Sunday: Sausage and Cheese Platter

Salami and cheese sandwich circles　*Cooked Cumberland sausage on a*
Ham sausage with grilled cheese tops　*thick slice of sauté potato*
Cheese-stuffed tomatoes　*Bacon-wrapped chipolatas*
　Grape-garnished cheese fingers

Place a line of cheese-stuffed tomatoes down the centre of your platter.
On the right of this arrange a line of Cumberland sausage on sauté
potato. On the left-hand side put a line of bacon-wrapped chipolatas alternating with salami and cheese sandwich circles. Repeat these last lines but
reverse the sides. Border your platter with an edge of ham sausage with
grilled cheese on top, interspersed with grape-garnished cheese fingers.
Garnish with bunches of watercress and celery leaves.

SALAMI AND CHEESE SANDWICH CIRCLES

Cut a 2in circle from a slice of Cheddar or similar cheese. Spread both
sides lightly with English mustard. Sandwich it between two slices of 2in
salami.

HAM SAUSAGE WITH GRILLED CHEESE TOPS

Cut ¼in thick slices of ham sausage. Cover thickly with grated cheese and
toast under the grill.

CHEESE-STUFFED TOMATOES

Cut the tops from firm tomatoes. Scoop out a little pulp and season
with salt, pepper and a little sugar. Partly cook in the oven. Fill with grated
cheese mixed with a little minced or grated onion. Finish under the grill.

COOKED CUMBERLAND SAUSAGE ON SAUTE POTATO

Parboil thick slices of potatoes (the waxy ones are best). Sauté in butter and then sprinkle with coarse salt. Place a thick slice of cooked Cumberland sausage on top and secure with a cocktail stick.

BACON-WRAPPED CHIPOLATAS

(See page 33).

GRAPE-GARNISHED CHEESE FINGERS

Cut a small finger of cheese. Spread lightly with mild mustard, sprinkle with minced or grated radish and garnish with halves of black and green grapes.

Third Sunday: Hot Dogs *(allow four to six per person)*

Have a large basket of miniature Hot Dogs made with 3in bridge rolls and pork chipolata sausages. The rolls must be ordered for Saturday and kept moist by covering with a damp cloth. Buy the chipolatas, 16 to the pound, and twist each one into two. (This is cheaper than buying the cocktail-sized ones). Cook them in deep fat, still in strings, in a wire basket. Have a big pan of oil or lard. Put it on the heat and allow it to warm through just enough to melt the fat. Then put in the wire basket full of sausages. Let the heat increase very gradually but watch carefully that the sausages do not darken too much in colour. They will take about 15 to 20 mins to cook in this way and will not burst. When they are cooked, drain on crumpled paper. Split the rolls. Spread one side with mild English mustard. Put a hot sausage in each one. Cover with kitchen foil and keep hot.

Fourth Sunday: Stuffed Sausage Platter

This is a really substantial one for you; use large English pork sausages eight to the pound. Cook the sausages and stuff with one of the following fillings:

1. Split the sausages and sandwich thin slices of Cheddar cheese, spread with horseradish cream, in between the halves.

2. Split the sausages and spread with spicy chutney.

3. Split the sausages and fill with a crisp slice of cooked streaky bacon, sprinkled with chopped mushrooms which have been cooked in the bacon fat.

4. Half split the sausages and pipe in a filling of cream cheese mixed with tomato purée and decorate with cocktail onions.

Place these in neat rows and garnish with pickled cucumbers or gherkins. For presentation, see instructions for First Sunday (page 50).

Champagne party for that potentate feeling (2)

At least once in a lifetime everyone should give a champagne party. It is a splendid morale-booster and fits a special celebration better than anything. Lordly merchants assure us that 11 a.m. is the best time to drink it. So what about one enchanted Sunday morning?

There should be a sense of occasion about this party. Silver should gleam and glass sparkle. This is an Invitation party as opposed to the Dropping-In party.

We plan here for 30 people and for your champagne party for this number you will need at least 15 bottles in the house for your peace of mind, whichever way you serve the champagne. Talk to your wine merchant about it. He will supply it on "sale or return" but will not expect to have wet bottles without labels returned. Do not, therefore, stand too many bottles on ice. Allow $\frac{1}{3}$ of a bottle a person and that can go on ice, then your reserve bottles will be in good condition to return if necessary.

HOW TO ICE YOUR CHAMPAGNE

Unless you empty your refrigerator completely you will not be able to put in all the bottles, so it will be necessary to buy some ice. As this is Sunday there is a small problem, but it can be overcome. Buy the ice as late as possible on Saturday, put it into a metal bath in the coolest place and cover it with thick sacking. It might melt before the party but this doesn't matter. The water will be cold. The difference is that if this does happen you will need to stand your bottles in the icy water for a longer time than if you were standing them on the ice.

TO OPEN THE BOTTLE WITH NONCHALANT EASE

First remove the gold foil round the cork and examine the wire which holds the cork in position. There is a little twisted loop; untwist this (usually anti-clockwise) to loosen the wire. Put a napkin over the cork, hold the bottle by the neck in one hand and ease off the cork with the other. It may need quite a bit of pressure. When the cork comes out, hold the bottle at an angle of 45 deg. to prevent the wine from gushing all over the place.

There are many well-known brands of champagne and all can be bought as either vintage or non-vintage. Most people are perfectly happy with non-vintage and the difference runs to several shillings a bottle. The word "Brut" on the bottle means that it is dry; "Sec", not quite so dry and "Doux" stands for sweet. "Sec" is the most popular.

Some of the well-known names are Heidsieck, Pommery, Moët et Chandon, Veuve Clicquot, Mumm, Krug, Bollinger, Lanson, Louis Roederer, Perrier-Jouet, Taittinger. There are many others, you must take your pick.

The champagne can be presented in many ways. Given here are:

> Pink champagne
> Black Velvet
> Buck Fizz
> Champagne cocktail
> Straight champagne

PINK CHAMPAGNE

Served in frosted glasses this is a pretty drink. Several of the firms make it. It has been a social success here for some years, since Princess Margaret's liking for it set the fashion. Frost each glass as follows: hold it by the stem, dip the rim first in lemon juice and then in castor sugar— this will give a lacy edge. The juice of two large lemons is enough to frost 24 glasses.

BLACK VELVET

This is a reviving drink, spectacular prepared in front of your guests as you—with a grand gesture—pour bottle after bottle into a large silver punch bowl. Then add a few bottles of good stout in the proportions of a pint of stout to each bottle of champagne, and serve.

BUCK FIZZ

To one bottle of champagne add the well-strained juice of six oranges. Serve very cold.

CHAMPAGNE COCKTAILS

To mix champagne cocktails you need for each one a small cube of sugar, one drop of Angostura bitters and a small measure of brandy. Fill up with champagne and float a thin slice of orange on top.

STRAIGHT CHAMPAGNE

You can serve this direct from the bottle. It is no more expensive to use magnums (a magnum is two bottles) and looks very grand. If any of your guests is feeling a bit frail, there will be a miraculous recovery shortly!

Many people consider that German, French and other sparkling wines make a good alternative drink for this type of party.

When every guest has a drink, a bottle can be wrapped in a napkin and taken round, topping up. This method can be used once with champagne cocktails, but after that you will need to make a fresh mixture.

The food

You don't need a big variety but the one or two things you have must be rather special. This is a party for the discriminating. A good choice might be:

SMOKED SALMON SANDWICHES in crustless brown bread and butter.

PÂTÉ OR TERRINE. Two or three days beforehand, make a good pâté or terrine. Serve it turned out on an attractive dish, surrounded by its own jelly. Fill little bread baskets with small triangles of hot toast, leaving guests to help themselves. You will need a pair of hands in the kitchen for toast-making.

For 30 guests allow . . .

50 champagne glasses or goblets
3 trays for serving

jugs for orange juice
plates for serving sandwiches

Thoughtful touch

A quarter-bottle for the host half an hour before the party!

7: DRINKS IN THE GARDEN

An English garden, a long, decorated drink and a warm soft summer evening—the ingredients for a perfect party. Give it for visitors from overseas or to welcome home and revive colonial servants on leave (don't ask me what to do if it rains, just hope that for once in a lifetime you have the three ingredients together).

Summer drinks have three obligations. In appearance they must be long, cool-looking and inviting. They must have a refreshing, tangy taste; and, perhaps most important of all, they must induce a sense of well-being.

A contrast to "kick"

This should be in direct contrast to the "kick" of the winter "short" which hits you like a bomb. But it is possible to turn short dynamic drinks into summery leisurely ones while still enjoying a familiar flavour.

First among the favourites is a Pimms cup. Decorative and delicious, it will enhance the appearance of your drinks table. Drape and swag (see page 10) your table in deep pink taffeta and catch up the swags with bunches of White Heart cherries and borage flowers. Stand your ready-prepared Pimms in tall glass jugs and arrange an old silver fruit or cake stand with an attractive assortment of fruits and leaves, and more borage blue among it. Under the table keep your refills of drink standing in a container of chipped ice.

Have 8oz goblets ready prepared with the garnish (sliced apple, cherries, cucumber and borage). It is not necessary to give a freshly-garnished glass for refills. After the first one, the glasses can be replenished by pouring straight from the jug.

There are two schools of thought on the subject of the actual strength of the drink. Normally, 8pts of lemonade will mix one bottle of Pimms. Some people prefer to make this stronger by cutting down on the lemonade. For a Pimms party for 14 people, to be on the safe side, order:
3 bottles of Pimms No 1 (gin base)
or 3 bottles of Pimms No 2 (whisky base)
or 3 bottles of Pimms No 3 (brandy base)
2doz pint bottles of lemonade. (These are not always easy to buy, so order well in advance).

More long cool drinks
(ounces are in all cases fluid ounces)

STRAWBERRY FRUIT CUP
(This makes about 24 servings)

This is taken from the German Bowle drink and can equally well be made with fresh peaches.

Into a large bowl put 1lb fresh strawberries or about six ripe peaches (the latter should be cut into slices). Pour over them a small glass of brandy and about 4oz of bar syrup (see page 59).

Allow to stand for two hours (the bowl should stand in a bed of ice). Finally add three bottles of chilled Moselle or Hock. Before serving, make it sprightly with a little soda water, or, if the cost doesn't matter, add a bottle of sparkling Hock.

GIN CRUSTA
(1 bottle of gin is enough for 14 half-pint drinks).

For each drink allow: 2oz gin, 1oz fresh orange juice, 1oz fresh lemon juice (lime juice is also suitable), ½oz grenadine, 1 teaspoonful bar syrup (see page 59), 4 cubes of ice, sliced cucumber, orange and lemon for garnishing, about 5oz soda water, castor sugar and lemon juice for frosting the glasses.

Mix together in a jug, gin, fruit juice, grenadine, bar syrup and ice, and allow to stand until very cold. Meanwhile frost the rim of a glass by dipping it first in lemon juice and then in castor sugar. Pour in the cocktail. Add soda to the glass and garnish with cucumber, lemon and orange slices.

CLARET CUP
(For 12 drinks).

1 bottle claret, 2oz brandy, 1 syphon soda water, bar syrup to taste (see page 59), 2oz fresh orange juice. Garnish of lemon balm, cucumber and sliced orange.

Chill all ingredients and combine. Add the garnish and serve at once.

WHISKY JULEP

(1 bottle of whisky—some people prefer Bourbon—makes 14 juleps).

For each drink allow: 2oz whisky, 2oz fresh lemon juice, 2 sprigs of mint which have been bruised by hammering with the back of a wooden spoon, 1oz or less bar syrup (see below), 4 cubes of ice, 3oz soda water, a few sprigs fresh mint.

Add whisky, lemon juice, mint, syrup and ice together and allow to stand in a half-pint glass until very cold. Have the soda water standing in a very cold place and immediately before serving remove the bruised mint, add soda and garnish with fresh sprigs of mint.

NON-ALCOHOLIC FRUIT CUP

(For 12 to 15 people).

1 tin peaches or apricots, 1 tin of pineapple, half a melon, 1 cucumber, juice of 6 lemons, 3 red apples, 3 bananas, bar syrup to taste, $\frac{1}{3}$ bottle grenadine, 3 syphons soda water, ice, water.

Cut the melon into cubes or balls and slice the cucumber, apples and bananas thinly. Mix the contents of the two tins of fruit together and then add the lemon juice along with the melon, apple, cucumber and banana slices.

Add the grenadine and then increase the bulk eight times by adding approximately three pints of water and three syphons of soda water.

Add a large piece of ice, allow to melt and then just before serving add several small cubes into which you have frozen cherries and mint leaves.

These cubes can be made in the ordinary ice cube container, the cherries and mint leaves being added just before the water begins to solidify. For clear ice, boil the water first.

BAR SYRUP

All the foregoing recipes require one essential ingredient—bar syrup. This method of sweetening is far superior to just adding sugar as it eliminates that certain "thinness" common to many badly-made drinks.

Melt 1lb castor sugar in a teacup of water very slowly over gentle heat, then simmer for a few minutes. Remove any scum from time to time. Allow it to cool. The syrup is now ready for use.

The food

Keep the food on the plain side—here the drinks are the decorative feature. Serve:

Baby profiteroles or small, unsweetened éclairs (see page 105) filled with creamed crabmeat. Assorted small shapes of brown bread and mushroom butter:

MUSHROOM BUTTER

INGREDIENTS: 1lb small button mushrooms; a little butter; 2 shallots; 1 clove garlic; juice of 1 lemon; parsley; chives; ½lb unsalted butter.

METHOD: Remove the stalks from the mushrooms and reserve the caps. Chop the shallots and sauté in butter for a few minutes—then add the chopped mushroom stalks and crushed garlic. Cook gently altogether for a further 5 mins. Season lightly.

Rub through a sieve or blend with the lemon juice in an electric liquidiser. Cream the unsalted butter and work in the mushroom mixture, adding the lemon juice if mixture has been sieved. When the butter is smooth and creamy, add the well chopped parsley and chives.

When preparing the bread and butter shapes, sauté the mushroom caps lightly. Spread butter on to bread cut into attractive shapes with small cutters and top with the mushroom caps.

Thoughtful touch

Unobtrusive tins of anti-midge spray and small containers of soothing lotion against the enterprising ones who get through the defences.

8: A PLAN FOR 80 GUESTS

Every girl deserves the wedding of her dreams, with a lovely, flattering background specially thought out for her. And home is the nicest place to have it. Hotels and hired rooms at best only contribute an anonymous atmosphere unless a great deal of work is put in.

Briefing for the reception planner

Do investigate the possibility of a marquee. It is astonishing how many people even the smallest one will hold. A garden measuring 40ft by 30ft will take a marquee measuring 30ft by 20ft. This will hold 80 guests for a buffet-type reception and the lowest price for one of this size is about £20 without a lining, and £40 with one. A gay striped lining is very decorative and is worth the extra cost. For really grand occasions there are some magnificent tents, but they are, naturally, not cheap. A marquee in winter presents no problem as the tent contractors use all sorts of clever tricks with heating and lighting. You will also need some matting laid down on the grass. Mention this when discussing your plan with them. They will come to see you, measure up and give an estimate. Consult a classified directory for names and addresses of marquee and tent suppliers.

Don't worry about flower-beds and shrubs which you think in the way. Nearly always they can be taken into the marquee and used as part of the decoration. If you decide against a marquee, follow the plan for a buffet lunch or supper party on page 72.

Background for the bride

When deciding upon a colour scheme take into account the tent lining and also the bridal colours. Decorate with the colour of the bridesmaids' dresses or use the colour of the bride's flowers. Alternatively, drape and swag the buffet table with a suitable pastel shade and decorate with little posies of flowers similar to the bride's bouquet. But don't forget that the bride is the leading lady and the background should emphasis this.

Draping the buffet table

Having decided on a colour scheme, see page 10 for instructions on draping. Details of how to make a bar are given on page 28. You should also have chairs and a few small petticoated tables (see page 13).

The cake (previously made or bought)

Why not have a separate table for the wedding cake? A 2ft circular table would be ideal. It could have a petticoat (see page 13) of lace, sprigged muslin or silk and be decorated with posies similar to the bride's bouquet and lover's knots of satin ribbon. Whether you buy or make the cake, you will need a silver cake-stand and knife. You can hire these from the firm who make the cake or from the local baker. It will cost between 15s and 30s.

Help for the hostess

The bride's mother, next in importance to the bride and groom, cannot manage a reception for 80 without help. A few pounds here on paid help would be money well spent. If this is not possible, some reliable relatives and family friends must be conscripted. At least two of them will need to forego the church in order to put last-minute touches to the buffet.

For 80 guests there must be at least 11 helpers—three to stand behind the buffet, three to ferry supplies and two for the kitchen. The other three helpers are for the bar.

The "barman"

One of the three bar helpers should be appointed as "barman". Go through the arrangements with him well before the wedding. Give him the entire drink to deal with. Don't bring in the Best Man for this, as he has other tasks. Let the amateur barman arrange with the wine merchant about deliveries, order the ice, check on the number of glasses, see that the drink is being properly chilled before he goes to church and be back in time to get the first drinks ready for the first guests. He will also be responsible for seeing that everyone has a full glass for the toasts. His two helpers will do the handing round of drinks.

Important points in your plan

1 Make sure that you have adequate space for the number of guests.

2 Check that you have borrowed or hired sufficient china, cutlery, and glass.

3 Check also on supplies of tea-towels, ashtrays and hand-towels. Every inch of cloakroom accommodation will be needed.

4 The more glasses you have the less washing-up during the reception.

5 Brief your helpers thoroughly, so that each knows what is expected of him.

Three-day timetable

THREE DAYS BEFORE assemble all materials for draping buffet, small tables, bar and wedding-cake table. Plan flower containers and order house and tent flowers.

TWO DAYS BEFORE, the marquee goes up. Start cooking and, if necessary, bring in your helpers.

EVE OF WEDDING see that all equipment is unpacked and check that you have sufficient of everything. This day will be the busiest in the kitchen. Your helpers can complete the food, all but for the final touches. Swag and drape the buffet table (see page 10) set up the bar (see page 28) and put out the glasses. Petticoat the wedding cake table. Arrange the cloths on the small tables and set them buffet-style with a fan of cutlery, groups of plates and folded paper napkins. If the bride's mother is doing flowers for the marquee, let her do them now, as she will be fully occupied on the day. Remember, the telegram boy will be calling all the time, the florist will be bringing bouquets and relatives will be arriving.

Put out the cat

Arrange for your pets to be boarded out. Don't forget, there will be lots of tempting food about.

Pack the cases

Help to pack the bride's going away clothes. The Best Man should then take the suitcase and the groom's to a safe place away from mischievous friends.

Important: If a marquee is being used, evening preparation is impossible if there is no artificial light. Have a long flex run from the house.

ON THE DAY put the final touches to the food. Arrange to have it ready in plenty of time before you go to church, leaving your Girls-Friday with clear instructions for last-minute jobs.

● ● ●

After the service

The bride's parents should leave the church immediately after the bridesmaids. They are the hosts at the reception and they must be there to welcome guests. They mustn't get trapped by friends and relatives they haven't seen for a long time. They can talk to them at the reception.

Announcing the guests

If guests are to be announced and a professional toastmaster is not being employed, delegate the job to a level-headed friend. All he needs to do is to ask the guests their names and repeat them clearly so that the hosts can hear. He need not shout them all over the place.

Receiving the guests in marquee or house

The bride's mother stands next to the door with her husband on her other side. Next come the bride and groom, with the bride standing next to her father, and, if there's space, the bridesmaids standing behind her. Then come the parents of the bridegroom, his mother next to him.

The guests are announced and move along the line offering their congratulations. There should be an uninterrupted flow, no-one should be allowed to stand and chat. The onus rests on the hosts who should follow Queen Elizabeth, the Queen Mother's gracious way of turning to the next comer. Immediately guests have been received, the "waiters" should be ready with trays to offer them a drink.

The telegrams

There is a move to reduce the number read at the reception. The Best Man reads those he has selected as the most interesting or amusing, making it a preliminary call to cut the cake. The reading gives time for the "waiters" to see that all glasses are full for the toasts.

The toasts

With a buffet-style reception, up to one hour is usually sufficient time to allow for the refreshments. Then the telegrams are read, the cake is cut and the toasts proposed. The usual toasts are first: "The bride and groom;" proposed by an old friend or relative of the bride's family. The bridegroom replies and finishes his speech by proposing the health of the bridesmaids. The Best Man replies on their behalf and if liked he can propose the health of the bride's parents. This is not absolutely necessary but it is nice. The bride's father replies (he always says he won't but usually makes the best speech of all). The cake can be cut either before or after the toasts. It should then be taken away into the kitchen and cut up. It is served as soon as the toasts are over.

After the cake-cutting and the toasts the bride and groom should move round, talking to guests. They should leave to change not longer than two hours after the beginning of the reception. (This is a good time for the helpers to serve a cup of tea). When they are ready, everyone waves them off and most people then prepare to leave.

Provide for the "back-room" people

You may have to provide something to eat and drink for chauffeurs, road patrol scouts and the local police, so arrange to have some beer and substantial sandwiches. Tea, as well.

Two wedding menus

For two wedding menus turn to page 65. The first is for a substantial buffet meal to take the place of lunch for a late morning wedding. The other is for the afternoon wedding reception, remembering that many guests will only have had a snack lunch in order to arrive on time.

continued on page 65

WEDDING LUNCH

The menu for 80 guests

Iced melon
Mousse of salmon in cucumber
mould
Chicken, almond and grape salad
Whole sugared ham

Cucumber salad
Strawberries, raspberries or fresh
fruit salad. Fresh cream
Strawberry pyramids
Coffee, hot or iced. Tea

The drinks

Assess quantities by calculating six glasses to a bottle.
Champagne: non-vintage or vin-tage

Sparkling white wine
Claret cup (see page 58)

The recipes

MOUSSE OF SALMON IN CUCUMBER MOULD

Made in 10 ring moulds. When turned out the top half is of jellied cucumber, the lower half of salmon mousse. First make the cucumber jelly.

INGREDIENTS FOR 80: 10 large cucumbers; 2 tablespoonsful white vinegar; juice of 3 or 4 lemons or to taste; seasoning; 7 tablespoonsful of aspic crystals; a little green colouring if needed.

METHOD FOR CUCUMBER JELLY: Peel cucumbers and grate finely. Measure and make up to 10pts with water. Add the seasoning, vinegar and lemon juice. Dissolve the aspic crystals in a little boiling water and add. Colour if necessary. Pour into 10 well-oiled ring moulds and leave to set.

Now make the salmon mousse base.

INGREDIENTS FOR 80: 20lbs cooked salmon, fresh, frozen or tinned; 4pts thick cream; 1½pts mayonnaise; juice of 8 lemons; 6oz aspic crystals dissolved in 1½pts of boiling water; seasoning; 8 tablespoonsful vinegar.

METHOD FOR SALMON MOUSSE: Skin and bone the salmon and mash or sieve finely. Mix in the mayonnaise and season well. Add vinegar, lemon juice and aspic. Lightly fold in the cream which has been whipped slightly (beware of over-beating). When the cucumber moulds are set divide the salmon mixture and spoon it on to the cucumber jelly. Drop the moulds very sharply on to the table several times to get a smooth finish. Put to set. When ready to serve, turn out on to platters. The centres may be garnished with asparagus tips or lettuce heart leaves.

CHICKEN, ALMOND AND GRAPE SALAD

For recipe see "A Chicken in Party Style," page 17. The flesh from six large boiling fowls will be required.

SUGARED HAM

INGREDIENTS: 1 gammon (12-15lbs); 3 tins peach halves; 3 tins pine-apple rings; 1lb demerara sugar; lettuce hearts.

METHOD: Stand the gammon under a running cold water tap for one hour. Place in a large saucepan with the juice from the 6 tins of fruit with sufficient water added to cover. Reserve the fruit for garnishing. Boil for 17 mins to each lb. When cool enough to handle remove the skin. Score the fat in an even criss-cross pattern with a sharp knife then press the sugar well into the cuts, covering the whole ham thickly. Put into a baking tin and bake at Gas Reg. No. 4 (358 deg. F.) until the sugar has formed a thick, crisp crust. Put the fruit in another tin keeping each piece flat, pour over a little of the liquid from the ham tin and cook it also in the oven for about 20 mins. To serve, put a ham frill on the bone end and cover ham with the fruit, fastening each piece on to the ham with a cocktail stick. Garnish with lettuce hearts.

CUCUMBER SALAD

You will need 6 cucumbers for this. Peel, slice finely, dress with French dressing and sprinkle with chopped parsley and chives.

FRESH FRUIT OR FRUIT SALAD

You will need 20lbs fruit and 8pts fresh cream.

STRAWBERRY PYRAMIDS

If you find the idea of making this quantity of meringue overwhelming, you might persuade your friends or the baker to make it for you. Failing this, the 10 eight-inch bases can be dispensed with and a Victoria sandwich cake base used instead. For this, follow the recipe for Easter Bunny cake (page 88).

Meringue will keep successfully for several days in air-tight tins, so the making can be spread over a good period, using your oven whenever it is free.

INGREDIENTS: 32 egg-whites; 4lbs castor sugar; 8lbs strawberries, fresh or frozen; extra sugar if necessary; 6pts thick cream, whipped.

METHOD: Spread the making over several days. Make a stiff meringue with the egg-whites and castor sugar. With this pipe 10 rounds about 8ins across on to oiled paper on baking sheets. Pipe round and round in decreasing circles until you have filled in the rounds. These make the bases for the pyramids. Pipe 10 similar rounds of 6ins and 10 of 3ins. With the rest of the mixture pipe very small 1½in wide meringues. Put all these into a very slow oven Gas Reg. No. ¼ (200 deg. F.) for about 1½ hours or until set and dry. On the day, cover the large bases with some of the strawberries mixed with sugar and a little of the whipped cream. Cover with a layer of the baby meringues. On top of these place the 6in size; build up again with strawberries, cream and small meringues. Then add the 3in base; cover with more fruit and cream and little meringues. Pipe large rosettes of cream all around. Decorate with the rest of the whole strawberries and sprigs of mint.

ICED COFFEE FOR 80

INGREDIENTS: 12pts of strong coffee. (Use 1½lbs freshly ground coffee); about 1lb sugar; 12pts milk; cream for topping, if liked.

METHOD: Bring the coffee almost to the boil and add the sugar. Allow to cool then add the milk. Stand on ice until very cold. Iced coffee is very good served with a little whipped cream floated on the top.

The equipment

160 Paris goblets or champagne glasses
80 goblets for iced coffee
7 service trays for handing drinks
120 small plates
120 fish plates
120 forks
100 dessertspoons
12 tablespoons for serving
80 teacups, saucers and spoons

7 two-pint teapots
7 hot water jugs
7 sugar basins
7 cream jugs
1 five-gallon water boiler
large jugs for iced coffee
wedding cake stand and knife
100 thick paper napkins
ashtrays unlimited

●   ●   ●

AFTERNOON WEDDING

The menu

160 hot lobster bouchées (see bouchées on page 31)
160 hot chicken bouchées
350 assorted sandwiches (smoked fish, honey and nut, minced ham, pâté and so on. To make roly-poly sandwiches, see page 89 and for additional sandwich fillings, see page 106)

100 asparagus tips rolled in thin brown bread and butter (see banana rolls, page 88)
80 small meringues
80 fresh fruit tartlets
80 chocolate and coffee éclairs
80 orange sponge cake slices (use sponge mixture given for Easter Bunny cake page 88)
Tea

The drinks
(Same as for Wedding Lunch)

The equipment

160 Paris goblets or champagne glasses
7 service trays for handing drinks
80 tea plates
80 tea cups and saucers and spoons
1 five-gallon water boiler
7 two-pint tea pots

7 hot water jugs
7 sugar basins
7 cream jugs
wedding cake stand and knife
pretty plates and platters
100 tea napkins
ashtrays unlimited

Making the tea

For this number of people a water-boiler is essential. Hire one (the local hall often has one, or you can, of course, go to a caterer). A 5-gallon one will provide enough water for 160 cups of tea and 1pt of milk will be needed for every 20 cups.

Tea bags are very useful for large numbers—otherwise the amount of tea leaves you have to dispose of is quite staggering. For every 2pt tea-pot, where quality counts, use 6 teaspoonsful of tea or 4 tea bags and make fresh when that is used. Where price decides, you can re-fill the pot with boiling water; that is, use the tea or tea bags twice. You will need to have at least 2lbs tea in hand to be on the safe side.

9 : WINE AND CHEESE PARTY

Blueprint for 40 guests

A wine and cheese party is an excellent way of entertaining a large number of guests both economically and conveniently. Because of these two virtues, however, it is sometimes a party that doesn't quite come off.

But it can be very enjoyable. The arrangements are similar to those for a cocktail party (see page 27) but substituting for spirits a good choice of drinkable wines served at the proper temperatures and an imaginative display of cheese and cheese dishes for the usual cocktail snacks.

The ideal time of day

My ideal wine and cheese party is given at about midday. There is a choice of two or three red wines, one or two white, one rosé and a sparkling wine. Beautifully garnished platters are dotted about the room and there is an ample supply of fresh glasses.

From time to time appetising hot tit-bits make their appearance (such as the hot cheese fritters, for which I give the recipe on page 70).

Take time with the platters

The platters and dips are worth taking time to prepare. They can be garnished with all kinds of fruits and vegetables (see page 18), which can be used for dipping into the cheese mixtures. Anyone who has admired the *corbeille des crudités* of a French hors d'oeuvres table will understand the value of red apples, celery curls, radish roses, baby carrots and various nuts. Try peeled walnuts sprinkled with salt and served hot from the oven. Fresh pineapple can also be used, as can chicory. The cheese dips (see page 70) can make a decorative centrepiece. Arrange them in small scooped-out pineapple halves and put them on a large silver tray.

The wines

For 40 guests you should allow about 20 bottles of wine. The white and rosé should be served chilled and the red should stand in the room for an hour or so with the corks drawn. I suggest Anjou rosé; a white sparkling Anjou, (Bouvet-Ladubay); Brauneberger (a Moselle); Lynch Bages or St. Emilion (Clarets); and Nuits St. Georges or Vosne Romanée (Burgundy).

The food

For the cheese side of the party you should allow two to three ounces for each guest. In addition, there should be dips and hot finger food.

All the English country cheeses are suitable. The firm-textured cheeses like Cheddar, Dunlop and Double Gloucester can be cut into fingers or cubes and allied to fresh grapes or pineapple. The crumbly cheeses, such as Lancashire and Cheshire, are best left in the piece, small plates, knives and table napkins lying conveniently near.

French cheeses do very well, of course, with French wines. A whole Brie would be delicious, and Ambassadeur, although rather strong in smell, is of just the right texture for handling. My suggested list of cheeses is: Brie; Ambassadeur; Grape cheese; Red Cheshire; Cheddar; Double Gloucester; Wensleydale and Stilton.

If you want to make a tremendous impact, a bowl of little home-made brown crusty rolls would put you right in the top class.

The recipes

HOT CHEESE FRITTERS

INGREDIENTS for the batter: 4 tablespoonsful plain flour; 1 dessertspoonful baking-powder; salt; 1 tablespoonful vinegar.

INGREDIENTS for the cheese mixture: 2 parts grated Parmesan cheese to 1 part well-creamed potato; a little made English mustard; fat for frying.

METHOD for the batter: Mix the flour with the salt and baking-powder. Add sufficient tepid water to mix to a smooth batter. Allow to stand for a few minutes and then add the vinegar. Mix well. This makes a crisp batter and does not go soft even when reheated.

To make the cheese mixture, blend together the grated cheese and potato, then add the mustard. Roll into small balls, dip into the batter and fry in deep, smoking fat.

The cheese dips

AVOCADO CREAM

Beat together sieved cottage cheese and one or two peeled avocado pears. Season well and add a tablespoonful of horseradish sauce strained through muslin. Add the juice of a lemon. The mixture should be light and creamy.

LIPTAUER

Mix 8oz cream cheese with a whole grated cucumber. Season with salt, pepper, cayenne and a good sprinkling of paprika and caraway seeds. A little anisette can be added with advantage. Beat until creamy and smooth.

BLUE CHEESE

To two parts of cream cheese and one part of whipped cream, add one part of well-mashed Danish Blue. Beat well together until smooth.

PINEAPPLE AND COTTAGE CHEESE

Combine coarsely-chopped fresh pineapple with a little freshly-whipped cream. Add to it twice the quantity of sieved and well-beaten cottage cheese. Put in a little Cointreau or Kirsch.

GARLIC CHEESE DIP

Put into a basin six portions of lactic cheese of the demi-sel variety. Add the juice from a pressed clove of garlic. Add salt, pepper and cayenne and pour in the top of two pints of milk. Beat very well together until light and fluffy.

10: SUMMER FORK PARTIES

LUNCH OR SUPPER PARTY FOR 40 TO 60 GUESTS

As I have planned this as a summer party, arrangements should be elastic. The ideal setting is a terrace or garden but the possibility of bad weather, alas, must be considered.

Three weather-wise plans

(a) Place your buffet table on the terrace, preferably covered by an awning fixed by the local tent people (see page 15). Guests help themselves and then eat indoors—one in the eye for the weather.

(b) Have the buffet table inside and, weather permitting, small tables outside. These can be brought in again if necessary.

(c) Have the buffet table on the terrace and small tables in the garden if the weather is really hot. If this is an evening party, don't forget the anti-midge spray. If flies are a hazard, cover all food lightly with damp greaseproof paper. Take it off as the first guest arrives.

If you have no garden and no terrace, clear the heavy furniture and fill your rooms with cool flowers and leaves, such as white syringa, white roses, white rhododendrons, stripped lime and spreading beech leaves. Have a buffet table in lemon or lime green and, if the party is in the evening, only candlelight. Drinks should be frosted and tinkling with ice. Food should be light and pretty as a picture. Provide ample seating accommodation. Small tables and chairs can be hired. Circular tables are the most convenient— a 3ft circular table will seat six guests comfortably. For full effect petticoat them (see page 13) in the same shade as the buffet table.

The menu

Cold asparagus with	*Peaches flamed in brandy,*
Mayonnaise Chantilly	*or strawberries Romanoff*
Crab mousse	*Small rolls*
Chicken salad in aspic	*Coffee*

The drinks

Meursault, Montrachet, or Pouilly Fuissé if your preference is a white Burgundy, but a Goldtroepfschen from the Moselle would be a charming choice. These can be served as apéritifs also.

The equipment

Several 3ft circular tables, depend-
ing on how many you wish to seat
at the same time
A corresponding number of chairs
3 service trays
1 block of ice
60 to 90 fish- or pudding-sized
plates
60 to 90 tea plates
40 to 60 small fruit dishes
80 to 120 small forks
40 to 60 dessertspoons

12 large serving spoons and forks
40 to 60 coffee cups and saucers
and spoons
80 to 120 Paris goblets to be used
for pre-lunch or supper drinks as
well as table wine
3 large coffee trays*
3 coffee pots
3 cream jugs
3 sugar basins
Ashtrays
3 sets pepper and salt

*It will be easier to serve coffee at tables.

The recipes

MAYONNAISE CHANTILLY

Mix equal quantities of very well-seasoned home-made mayonnaise (see page 41) (or there are one or two good commercial brands) and lightly-whipped fresh cream. For 40 people you will need about 1pt of each. Use fresh, tinned or frozen asparagus. Allow six to eight spears per person.

CRAB MOUSSE

These quantities make eight to 10 servings. Multiply accordingly—three or four times should be ample.

INGREDIENTS: 1lb crabmeat (this can be bought by the pound from multiple fishmongers); ½ cup mayonnaise; 1 tablespoonful brandy; 1 cup double cream; salt; cayenne pepper; 1oz powdered gelatine; juice of 2 lemons; 2 egg-whites.

METHOD: Pound the crabmeat. Add mayonnaise and brandy. Whip the cream until it just thickens and fold in. Over-whipping may lead to curdling. Season. Dissolve the gelatine in the hot lemon juice.

Allow to cool and stir lightly into the mixture. In fact this dish needs a very light touch throughout. Fold in the well-whipped egg-whites. Pour into an oiled soufflé dish and put in a cool place to set.

If liked, a little liquid aspic may first be poured into the bottom of the dish and allowed to set before the mixture is added. The aspic may be decorated with attractive small shapes of cucumber and tomato. To serve, turn out and garnish with chicory spears (see page 19).

CHICKEN SALAD IN ASPIC

You will need the flesh from 2 or 3 large boiling fowls and a variety of suitable moulds.

Decorate the bottom of a mould with small, green peas and circles of cucumber or tomato. Pour a little liquid aspic over and allow to set. Proceed to fill the mould with cooked chicken flesh cut into small cubes, interspersed with small strips of red and green peppers, seasoning with salt, pepper and a little grated onion as you go. When the mould is full, pour into it as much liquid aspic jelly (made according to the instructions on the packet, but substituting white wine for one-third of the quantity of liquid called for) as the mould will take. In warmer weather you can make firmer jelly by adding a little less liquid to the aspic crystals. Put into a cool place overnight to set.

Turn out on to a platter, garnish with lettuce hearts, watercress and tomato roses. For tomato roses, see page 21.

PEACHES FLAMED IN BRANDY

The yellow-fleshed, cheap Italian peaches are quite suitable for this dish. Poach the whole peaches gently in sugared water (1 part sugar to 2 parts water) for 3 to 5 mins. Remove from liquid, cool slightly and remove skins. Cut in half and take out stones.

When ready to serve, place cut side down in an ovenproof dish. Put into a hot oven or over a flame for a minute or so to get the serving dish really hot. Heat the required amount of brandy (about 1 tablespoonful per whole peach) in a pan or chafing dish. At the last minute, take the hot platter of peaches and the pan of near boiling brandy to the table. Pour a little brandy over each peach half and set alight immediately. Serve as many as possible while still flaming and hand separately brandy-flavoured, sweetened whipped cream.

SMALL LUNCH FOR 12 GUESTS

Normally this is a very feminine gathering, quite often a figure-conscious one at that. A hostess who is not over-lavish with the calories, while still presenting an interesting and appetising meal, will find her efforts appreciated.

The setting for this party should be smart and rather formal, with the best that the china and linen cupboards can produce. Here is a chance for the hostess to show her skill in flower arrangement as well as in other details. In fact, the party can be a charming combination of food and flowers.

You may like your menu to carry out the idea of your flower arrangement. Here I suggest two schemes, complete with recipes.

1 Lime green and white—this colour combination always looks cool and attractive.

2 A blue and green scheme—massed blue flowers are a new trend in decoration and the food can have a green theme garnished with blue.

1 : LIME GREEN AND WHITE PARTY

To get a delicate lime shade for a smart table covering, a double layer of green net or nylon thrown over a primrose yellow cloth is just right. Or a hostess who means to take this job seriously could easily copy some of the pretty Italian cloths: a coarse white linen one, with clusters of fruit cut from lime green material and appliquéd on to it would look delightful. Have green-stemmed wine glasses as well.

The flowers

This cool summer arrangement is lightly outlined with sprays of stripped lime that contrast with the bold shape of the shaded funkia leaves. These, set low, throw into relief the Auratum lilies, the centre of the group. The slender lines of a few white flag irises still in bud, and some pale acid yellow Ester Reid daisies complete the picture. If lilies and irises are not obtainable white peonies and campanulas may be used instead.

1 *Stripped lime*
2 *Flag irises*
3 *Ester Reid daisies*
4 *Auratum lilies*
5 *Funkia leaves*

The menu

Platter of young raw vegetables
Prawns in a cucumber mould
Chicken and ham chaud-froid with
braised pineapple
Sorbet-filled mandarins

Starch-reduced rolls for the dieters
Toasted "pulled" bread for the
fortunates. Butter
Coffee—hot or iced

The apéritif

There are those who do not care for spirits during the day. A white
Cinzano with a little soda, a thin slice of lemon and a little ice makes a
most pleasant apéritif.

The wine

Alsatian (Gewürztraminer) or Moselle (Piesporter Goldtroepfschen). Arrange for the delivery of the wine the preceding day and stand it either in
the refrigerator or in the kitchen sink containing a few pieces of ice for an
hour before using. White wine does not need decanting—it can be served
direct from the bottle.

The recipes

PLATTER OF YOUNG RAW VEGETABLES

Arrange a selection of washed, tender young vegetables in a trug or on a
platter. Lettuce hearts, tiny carrots, fennel, asparagus, spring onions,
radishes, young beans and so on.

Serve with several different dressings: for example, vinaigrette, tarragon, mustard or lemon (guests help themselves and make their own
salads).

PRAWNS IN A CUCUMBER MOULD

INGREDIENTS: 2 large cucumbers; about 1pt water; white vinegar and
lemon juice to taste; seasoning; a little green vegetable colouring; 2oz
powdered gelatine; two 1lb packs of frozen prawns; French dressing.

METHOD: Peel and finely grate the cucumbers. Measure and make up to
2pts with water. Dissolve the gelatine in a little hot water, add to the
cucumber liquid. Add seasoning and lemon juice to taste. Colour if necessary. Pour into two oiled ring moulds. Put into refrigerator to set. To
serve, turn out and fill the centres with prawns dressed with a little
French dressing.

CHICKEN AND HAM CHAUD-FROID WITH
BRAISED PINEAPPLE

INGREDIENTS: 18 slices cooked chicken breast; 18 similar sized slices of
cooked ham (about ¼in thick); 1½pts Béchamel sauce; ½oz gelatine; ½pt of
made aspic; seasoning; ½pt cream; 1 tin pineapple rings; watercress;
cucumber peel; little lemon rind.

METHOD: Place a chicken slice on top of a ham slice and trim to get a
good shape. While the Béchamel sauce is still warm, add the gelatine dissolved in a little of the hot aspic. Season very well (plenty of pepper). Add
the cream. Strain if necessary. Keep stirring while the sauce is cooling.

Coat the chicken and ham slices with the sauce. See that every bit is evenly covered. When set, pour over each piece a little of the remainder of the aspic which has been allowed to get to the point of set. Now garnish each piece of chicken with long thin strips of cucumber peel and little diamonds of lemon peel. Arrange the diamonds in the shape of a daisy with a cucumber strip as a stem. Drain the pineapple. Cut each ring into half and put into a baking tin, brush over with melted butter and sprinkle with demerara sugar. Bake at Gas Reg. No. 3 (336 deg. F.) for 30 mins. Dress the chicken and ham slices on a dish, garnish with watercress and make a border with the halved pineapple rings.

SORBET-FILLED MANDARINS

INGREDIENTS: 12 mandarin or tangerine oranges; 1½pts lemon sorbet (if unobtainable, use ice-cream); castor sugar.

METHOD: Cut a little lid from each orange. Carefully scoop out the flesh. Put skins into cold water to soak for a few hours. Then with a teaspoon scrape away the pith. Keep the skins whole. Dip into water and then roll in the castor sugar. Put into the refrigerator until ready to fill. Just before serving fill each orange with the sorbet. Put back the lid. Tuck a small white bloom, freesia, baby gladiola single bloom or a white daisy or marguerite under the lid with a small camellia leaf or other glossy small leaf. Serve on green glass or pottery plates.

TOASTED "PULLED" BREAD

METHOD: Immerse a sandwich loaf in hot water for 10 seconds and put it in a hot oven for a few minutes. Cut off the long crust and pull out the soft crumb. Divide this into rocky looking pieces by pulling it into hunks lightly and quickly with the fingers of both hands. Place the pieces of bread on a baking sheet and bake them again until very pale gold. The "pulled" bread should be quite crisp when cooked.

2: THE BLUE AND GREEN PARTY

Emphasise the contrast of dark blue and green by using a bottle-green cloth with gentian-blue linen table-napkins.

The menu

Cream cheese pears on lettuce hearts (garnished with borage flowers and small bay leaves)
Whole salmon trout — work and garnish as for whole salmon (page 24)
Mayonnaise verte
Toasted "pulled" bread

Mousse of fresh gooseberries (turned out like a charlotte russe and decorated with sponge fingers, crystallized or fresh violets and mint leaves, tied round in the old English way with a narrow dark blue ribbon)
Starch-reduced rolls. Butter
Coffee—hot or iced

The apéritif

As for lime green and white party.

The wine

Schloss Böckelheimer. This is a very pleasant German wine from the river Nahe district, usually acceptable to a feminine palate. It is slightly "spritzich".

The flowers

Set in a silver cake stand raised about 6ins above the table, this sophisticated arrangement of mixed blue flowers and no foliage forms an unusual buffet decoration. Slim, rather undersized spikes of delphinium (the second flowering is perfect) splay outwards at the sides. Scabious, nigella and cornflowers build up to a low rounded centre with blue hydrangea heads and a handful of brilliant dark gentians tucked in nearby. A trailing pendant of fragrant wisteria is slipped in at the last moment.

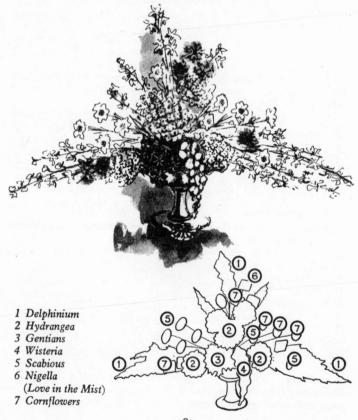

1 Delphinium
2 Hydrangea
3 Gentians
4 Wisteria
5 Scabious
6 Nigella
   (Love in the Mist)
7 Cornflowers

The recipes
CREAM CHEESE PEARS ON LETTUCE HEARTS

INGREDIENTS: 6 large ripe pears; ½pt cream; 12oz cream cheese; seasoning; lettuce hearts; a few green grapes; borage flowers; bay leaves.

METHOD: Peel, halve and core the pears. Whip the cream lightly and add to the cream cheese. Whip both together until light and fluffy. (Beat very gently, otherwise the cream will get curdy). Season well. Place the pear halves cut side down and mask each one with the cheese mixture. Put in a cold place for half an hour or so. Decorate a large platter with lettuce heart leaves and put the pears on them. Garnish each pear with whole or halved seeded grapes, a sprig of borage flower and a small bay leaf.

WHOLE SALMON TROUT

See page 24.

MAYONNAISE VERTE: Make a well-blended purée of cooked parsley, spinach and tarragon and add a little to your home-made mayonnaise.

MOUSSE OF FRESH GOOSEBERRIES

INGREDIENTS: Sponge fingers; 2pts well sweetened gooseberry purée; 2pts whipped cream; 4oz gelatine (dissolved in a little hot water); green vegetable colouring.

METHOD: Stir the gelatine well into the gooseberry purée while the purée is still warm. Allow to cool to blood heat and fold in the whipped cream. The mixture may need a touch of green vegetable colouring, but keep it a very pale green. Pour into two wetted soufflé dishes and put into the refrigerator to set. When firm, turn out and press the sponge fingers around the sides. Pipe with whipped cream and decorate with crystallised or fresh violets and mint leaves. Tie a blue ribbon round and finish with a bow.

The equipment

This is the same for both parties, except where an alternative number is given.

12 5oz goblets for the apéritif
12 hock or stemmed glasses
36 small meat plates
12 tea plates
12 butter knives
12 coffee cups and saucers
12 coffee spoons
24 knives for lime green and white party (none needed for blue and green)
36 small forks
12 ice-cream spoons (for lime green and white) or 12 dessert

spoons (for blue and green party)
2 coffee pots
2 sugar basins
2 cream jugs
1 large tray for coffee
1 tray for serving drinks
Ashtrays
Serving spoons and forks
Ice bucket (optional)
1 bucket of ice (from the fishmonger—optional)
Linen napkins
Platters or serving dishes

11:
CHRISTMAS
BUFFET

Christmas hospitality. What a heart-warming custom, with its two traditional approaches—"open house" right through the holiday period or one splendid all-out effort which, if well-planned, is undoubtedly the more satisfactory.

Here is a blueprint for a festive party for 30 guests, which can be given at any time during Christmas or the New Year.

The buffet table

This can be the year's most rewarding culinary operation, as housewives can justify a little extra extravagance and most cooks are in the mood. If much of the food can be prepared in advance, they can afford to spend a certain amount of time on decorating and dressing the table itself.

One of the prettiest I have ever done had a gathered three-tiered flounce in white muslin sprigged with red. The table top was covered in red sateen and the centrepiece was a pyramid of Christmas roses, holly, mistletoe and little red velvet bows (sketched above).

Cut a piece of 1½in-mesh chicken wire about 18ins by 24ins. Bend this into a cone shape about 12ins high with a base of 9ins in diameter. By turning in the surplus 6ins in height, you make a firm rounded edge to the base. Twist the wires at the tip of the pyramid to a fine point.

Sprig this cone shape with holly, mistletoe, a few Christmas roses and red velvet bows. (Put these into place with florists' wire). If you use artificial Christmas roses for this, the arrangement will then last for many days.

The food

This should be a careful balance between "trad" and modern—all the old favourites should be there but with new and interesting presentation. Turkey? By all means. Mince pies, too. And whoever heard of Christmas without roast pork, or oranges for that matter? But these all cry aloud for a bit of imagination.

Very well, then. Boil the turkey in a flavoursome stock which afterwards you will reduce and reduce until you have a succulent jelly. Serve the bird in easily-handled pieces which are embedded in the delicious stuff. A boned joint of pork can be stuffed with prunes and whole Frankfurter sausages, and when you carve it each slice will be dotted with appetising circles of sausage and juicy prunes. Make your mince pies, but leave off the lid and instead put a spoonful of lemon icing on to the mincemeat. Turn a bowl of Christmas oranges into a gleaming white frosted pyramid, an edible table decoration.

The menu for 30 guests

Prawns in turtle aspic

Herring salad garnished with

eggs Diplomat

Jellied turkey

Glazed stuffed pork with cole slaw and jellied apples

Frosted orange pyramid

Yule log surprise

Apricot mousse

The recipes for 30

PRAWNS IN TURTLE ASPIC

INGREDIENTS: 3 1lb packs of Norwegian frozen prawns; 3 tins turtle soup; 3 tins clear consommé; 6 dessertspoonsful aspic crystals; juice of 3 lemons; 6 tablespoonsful sherry.

METHOD: Defrost the prawns and divide into two large serving dishes. Melt the turtle soup and consommé until near boiling point. Dissolve the aspic crystals in a little boiling water and add to the soup, together with the lemon juice and sherry. Stand in a cold place until on the point of setting, then pour on to the prawns. Stir several times to distribute the prawns. When set, turn out. Garnish with a border of shredded lettuce and lemon sections. Serve with small rolls of thin brown bread and butter.

HERRING SALAD

INGREDIENTS: 15 rollmop herrings; 15 large potatoes, peeled and boiled; 6 large beetroots, boiled and peeled; 8 large apples; 8 medium-sized onions; 8 pickled cucumbers; ½ cup vinegar; ½ cup sugar; 1 teaspoonful pepper; ¾pt cream.

METHOD: Cut the herrings into strips, dice the potatoes and beetroots, chop the apples, onions and pickled cucumbers. Mix well together. Add the vinegar, sugar and pepper to the cream. Whip and add to the salad. Chill for an hour or two before serving and garnish with eggs Diplomat.

EGGS DIPLOMAT

INGREDIENTS: 15 hard-boiled eggs; few slices smoked salmon; mayonnaise.

METHOD: Slice the eggs lengthwise. Remove the yolks and fill the cavities with shredded smoked salmon bound with a little well-seasoned mayonnaise.

JELLIED TURKEY

Roast cold turkey can be dry and uninteresting. By breaking away from tradition and boiling the bird the flesh stays moist and succulent.

INGREDIENTS: One 12 to 15lb turkey; two pig's trotters chopped into pieces; some good veal bones, well broken; four onions; few stalks of celery; bouquet garni (parsley, thyme, bayleaf); salt; pepper; ½ bottle dry white wine; clove of garlic; sherry; glass of brandy. Lettuce hearts, asparagus and tomatoes for garnishing.

METHOD: Prepare this dish at least one day before serving. Pull out any pieces of fat from the inside of the turkey and place the bird in a large pan with the trotters and veal bones. If your pan is not big enough, ask your butcher to cut the bird in half for you. Add the sliced onions, celery stalks, bouquet garni and seasoning. Pour in the wine and add the crushed clove of garlic (enough to flavour slightly). Add sufficient water to cover the bird. Cover and simmer gently for about 2½ to 3 hours or until tender, but not breaking away. Remove the bird from the pan and while it is cooling boil the liquid you have cooked it in very rapidly, skim and add the brandy. Cut the meat from the frame into large pieces and put into a deep bowl. When the stock has reduced by half, correct the seasoning and remove the bones. Skim any fat and strain the liquid over the pieces of turkey. Stand the bowl in a cold place until jelly is set. When ready to serve, the pieces of bird are carefully lifted out, keeping each one well coated with jelly. Garnish with lettuce heart leaves and small bundles of asparagus slotted through rings of tomato (see illustration on page 26).

GLAZED STUFFED PORK

INGREDIENTS: 6lbs loin of pork, boned; apple stuffing (see page 84); 24 large soaked stoned prunes; 12 Frankfurter sausages; salt and pepper; meat glaze (see page 84).

METHOD: Place the pork on the table with the narrow end towards you. Spread a layer of apple stuffing on to the meat. Arrange the sausages across the stuffing with the prunes dotted in between. Carefully roll up the loin, pinning the ends with skewers and tying the roll several times with string. Sprinkle with salt and pepper and roast at Gas Reg. No. 4 (358 deg. F.) for about 2½ to 3 hours. When cooked, place on a flat surface. Put a wooden board on top, with a 6lb weight on it. Stand in a cold place overnight. The next day, warm the joint slightly, wipe off surplus fat and remove the string and skewers. Coat with meat glaze—you may have to give it two or three coatings. Allow to set. To serve, slice thinly and garnish the platter with little mounds of cole slaw alternated with jellied apples standing on green leaves.

MEAT GLAZE: Few people nowadays, alas, can afford to make real glaze. Here is a satisfactory substitute: Melt one good tablespoonful aspic crystals in 1pt water. While still hot, add a tablespoonful of good meat extract and a small glass of sherry. Add sufficient gravy browning to colour it a rich deep brown. Mix 1 dessertspoonful cornflour with cold water, bring the aspic to the boil, pour on to the cornflour. Return to the pan and cook for a minute or two until it has thickened. Use on the point of set.

APPLE STUFFING

INGREDIENTS: 1lb cooking apples; 2 tablespoonsful water; 1oz sugar; 2oz butter; 4oz white breadcrumbs; 1 beaten egg; handful chopped parsley; seasoning.

METHOD: Peel and slice the apples and simmer until tender with the water, sugar and butter. Add the breadcrumbs and beaten egg and parsley. Mix well together. Season.

COLE SLAW

INGREDIENTS: 1 large firm white cabbage; salted water. Ingredients for the dressing: 2oz sugar; 1oz flour; ½oz dry mustard; ¼oz salt; 1oz butter; 2 egg-yolks; ½ cup vinegar; 1 cup cream.

METHOD: Shred the cabbage very thinly and stand overnight in cold salted water. Drain and dry very thoroughly.

METHOD FOR THE DRESSING: Mix sugar, flour, mustard and salt together in a basin. Stand over a pan of boiling water and add butter, egg-yolks and vinegar. Stir well until thick. Stand until cold, then beat in the cream. Pour it over the shredded cabbage and turn several times until well coated.

JELLIED APPLES

Peel and core small apples. Poach in sugar and water until cooked but still firm. Chill thoroughly. Over heat melt 1lb redcurrant jelly with a small glass of port wine, thicken with 2 teaspoonsful arrowroot slaked with cold water. Pour over the apples, coating them thoroughly. When set, give them another coating. Use as garnish for the pork.

APRICOT MOUSSE

INGREDIENTS: 2lbs dried apricots; 2 cups sugar; 4 tablespoonsful brandy; 4pts cream; 4oz powdered gelatine; 8 egg-whites; 8oz split almonds; icing sugar.

METHOD: Soak apricots overnight then simmer them in the same liquid until soft. Drain and rub through a sieve or purée them in an electric blender. Reserve the liquid. Add the sugar to the purée and cook over gentle heat until sugar is dissolved. Cool then add the brandy. Whip the cream until light and thick but not "curdy" and fold lightly into the purée. Melt the gelatine in some of the liquid from the apricots and add a little at a time, folding well into the mixture. Lastly whip the egg-whites and fold in also. Pour into oiled moulds or soufflé dishes and put into a cold place to set. Put the almonds on to a baking tray, sprinkle them with icing sugar and bake in a moderate oven, stirring and sprinkling them with the sugar frequently, until they are pale brown. When the mousse is set, decorate the top with the almonds.

FROSTED ORANGE PYRAMID

You will need to frost about 18 oranges. Choose small, well-shaped ones (sketched below).

INGREDIENTS FOR FROSTING: 4 unbeaten egg-whites; ½pt cold water; castor sugar.

METHOD: Mix egg-whites and water; peel the oranges, taking care not to break the inner skin. Brush each one all over with the egg-white mixture. Half-fill a baking tin with castor sugar, put in two or three of the prepared oranges at a time and shake the tin vigorously, rolling the fruit about until well-coated with sugar. Put on greaseproof paper to dry, and then give them another coating. You may even need to repeat this once more. After the final coating, dry well, turning the oranges once to dry the under side. You may frost a few grapes at the same time if liked (see instructions below).

To BUILD THE PYRAMID: Use a silver cake board about 9ins across, and cover with chicken wire, which should be secured firmly to the edges. Cover the wire with crumpled kitchen foil. Arrange an outer circle of frosted oranges, sitting the fruit well down on to the foil. Make another circle inside the first one and wedge one or two oranges into the centre cavity. Build another circle on top and continue, pyramid shape, for three or four layers. Stand the arrangement on a china or silver cake stand and decorate with silvered and frosted leaves. If liked, the spaces between the oranges can be filled in with a few green grapes. Use the same frosting method as for the oranges. For a special effect, complete the decoration with white freesia heads.

YULE LOG SURPRISE

You will need three or four of these. Cut both ends (about ½in thick) from a large, stale old-fashioned Swiss roll. (The pre-packed brands are too thin and moist for this recipe). With a long, thin knife, loosen the centre and ease it through. Spread one of the ends you have cut off with jam and stand the roll upright on to it. Pack with well-drained fruit salad. Place flat on a baking sheet and secure the other end back in place with a little jam. Make a stiff meringue (2oz castor sugar to each egg-white), pile it on to the roll and mould into shape with a fork. Put into a cool oven and bake at Gas Reg. No. 1 (291 deg. F.) until dry, but not brown. Add seasonal decorations if you like.

12: EASTER BUNNY PARTY

The Easter Bunny is a fleet-footed, early-rising character who races round the garden at dawn on Easter Sunday morning hiding little presents for children. Where I first learnt about this pretty continental custom I can't say but it was turned into an annual occasion in my own family.

He might put a box of coloured pencils in the apple tree, sweets among the wallflowers and a tiny doll in with the tulips. My children loved him better than Father Christmas, Big Bill Campbell or even Dick Barton. Several times they were sure they had caught a glimpse of him. It was a few years before they connected their eagerly-awaited visitor with mother's dew-soaked dressing-gown hanging to dry.

For 12 under-sevens

It is a joyous custom belonging to the loveliest time of the year, and can easily be used as a background for a children's party for under-sevens, the procedure remaining the same but the time changed to afternoon. The tinies will need a bit of help and there must be an adult to see fair play. The presents should be gaily wrapped and, if possible, all the same, to avoid disappointment.

The Easter Bunny table

Use a pale green or lemon tablecloth. Cut figures of rabbits or chicks out from paper or material and fix them on to the cloth with a paste that will wash off afterwards. Decorate cress punnets with fluffy chicks, primroses, violets and other spring flowers and a few tiny eggs. In the centre of the table have a decorated Easter Bunny cake (see page 88).

The menu for 12

(This allows for mummies, big sisters or the *au pair* girls who accompany or come to collect).

Iced Easter Bunny cake: 12 portions

Cumberland sausage ring: 12 portions

Chipolata sausages: 2lbs twisted into 64 small ones

Banana rolls: 36

Honey, apricot and nut roly-poly: 30 to 40 portions

Bunny biscuits: 24

Jellied orange quarters: 24

Small sandwiches: 48

Milk shakes: 6pts

Fruit drink: 9pts

The recipes

EASTER BUNNY CAKE

This is made from two Victoria sponges sandwiched together. To make these you need two sandwich cakes baked in 10in tins (½lb each of flour, sugar and butter and four eggs). Cream together the butter and sugar. Beat in the eggs one at a time. Sieve the flour and fold in by hand. Do not beat. Divide the mixture between the two lined and greased 10in sandwich tins with straight sides. Bake in the middle of the oven at Gas Reg. No. 4 (358 deg. F) for 20 to 25 minutes. Sandwich together with lemon icing. Ice all over with white icing and decorate with milk chocolate rabbit shapes, yellow fluffy chicks, eggs and a posy of flowers.

CUMBERLAND SAUSAGE RING

For this you need ½lb of puff pastry and 1lb of Cumberland sausage. This unending roll is sold at many butchers', delicatessen shops and supermarkets. If unobtainable, then good pork sausage meat can be made into a roll 1½ins in diameter. Roll out the pastry into a long strip 5ins wide, and about 18ins long. Skin the sausage, then roll it with the palm of your hand to extend it to the same length as the pastry. Place it in the middle of the pastry and encase the sausage, brushing the joined edges with beaten egg. Put on a baking sheet with the joined edges underneath and shape the strip into a circle. Pinch the two ends well together at the join. Brush it with beaten egg and bake at Gas Reg. No. 7 (424 deg. F.) for 20 minutes.

CHIPOLATA SAUSAGES

Take 2lbs of pork chipolatas and twist each one in half to make a cocktail size. Cook them in the string (this is important) in hot fat, cut, put on sticks and spike them into a red apple. Place the apple in the centre of the Cumberland sausage ring for serving (see sketch on page 92).

BANANA ROLLS

Cut six bananas into three, then slice each piece through lengthwise, to make 36 pieces in all. Nine slices of thin brown bread are cut lengthwise from a half-quartern loaf. Decrust and cut through the middle lengthwise and then each half is cut in half again, making four oblong slices, about 4ins by 2ins. These are buttered, a piece of banana put on each, sprinkled with lemon juice and sugar and rolled up.

HONEY, APRICOT AND NUT ROLY-POLY

Use the remaining four or five slices of the half-quartern loaf. Butter and spread them first with a little honey and then with apricot jam. Sprinkle with chopped nuts. Roll up and wrap tightly in greaseproof paper and put in the refrigerator for an hour. Take off the paper and cut each roll into seven or eight pieces.

BUNNY BISCUITS

Cream 8oz of butter and 6oz castor sugar, and beat in one egg. Add the grated rind of a lemon. Sieve in 12oz plain flour and knead it all well together. Put in the refrigerator for an hour. Roll out thinly and cut out with a bunny-shaped biscuit cutter. Bake at Gas Reg. No. 4 (358 deg. F.), for about 20 mins. Dust with icing sugar.

JELLIED ORANGE QUARTERS

Cut six oranges in half lengthwise and scoop out the pulp and pith. Fill each half with a different colour of fruit jelly (made from a packet but using slightly less water) using one packet each of lemon, raspberry and lime. When it is set firmly, cut each piece in half lengthwise again and arrange like a sunflower on a platter. Assort the colours as you go.

SMALL MARMITE AND WATERCRESS SANDWICHES

Using one white loaf and one brown, cut 12 slices of each. This will give you 48 little sandwiches. Spread the bread with butter, Marmite and chopped watercress. Cut into triangular sandwiches.

MILK SHAKES

To each ½pt of milk add a small brick of ice-cream and a little fruit juice. Whisk and stand in the refrigerator.

FRUIT DRINK

Use the juice from tinned or bottled fruit. Add fizzy lemonade and garnish with fruit slices. Stand in the refrigerator.

A Thoughtful Touch: put a coloured "Dorothy" bag by each plate, to carry home the "loot". Make them from crêpe paper.

13:
CHILDREN'S
PARTIES

Time was when a children's party was a simple affair of dressing-up, coloured jelly and lots of prizes. As soon as the little darlings arrived, you clapped a tinsel crown on their curly topknots, fastened on fairy wings, put a silver wand in their hands and took them on a tour of the Enchanted Wood (up the stairs, in and out of the bedrooms and down again).

On the way they met with the usual adventures. The witch (dressed in an old party cloak) uttered a fearsome curse, but was banished by the Fairy Queen (Aunt Elaine in her ballet dress) who bobbed out of the bathroom glittering like a harvest moon.

A dark corner somewhere was disguised as the wood and of course there was the treasure in it and they all got a little present. By then it was tea-time and you were half-way through.

Today's young spacemen would consider that routine very old hat indeed, but I think you could get away with it for the babies. Five-year-olds will enter into a world of fantasy with a very serious face, but a single scathing remark from an eight-year-old can immediately make the whole thing seem ridiculous.

If you cannot help mixing the age-groups (and this is to be avoided if at all possible; a ganged-up trio of 10-year-olds can create havoc among the tinies) enlist adequate help and try to operate in two well-divided camps.

Party activities can be divided up like this:

FOUR, FIVE AND SIX-YEAR-OLDS

(The sixes only just fit into this group)

Let them act a fairy story told by a good story-teller. Appropriate "props" should be kept in readiness—crowns, wings, wands and so on. There should always be a "treasure" of some kind at the end. Gaily-wrapped identical small parcels could be discovered in an old treasure chest (any container suitably disguised). This will take you to tea-time.

Menu ideas

SANDWICH BOX

Cut small, easily recognisable sandwiches (egg, jam, honey, banana, Marmite—but NO mayonnaise) and pack them inside a scooped-out sandwich or tin loaf (sketched below). Cut the top crust off the loaf lengthwise to form the "lid" and scoop out the crumb. Line the "box" with lettuce leaves, then pile the sandwiches in. Prop the "lid" open with cocktail sticks to make it look like a chest.

*Pack the box with
small, easily
recognisable sandwiches*

PRETTY LITTLE CAKES

Victoria sandwich mixture, lemon-iced, cut into various very small shapes, decorated with piped names or initials, golliwog faces, animals, or baked in boat-shaped moulds and trimmed with paper sails. In this case, the boats must all have names, like Water Sprite, Saucy Sue, Jolly Roger, and so on.

CUMBERLAND SAUSAGE RING

For instructions, see page 88 (sketched below).

MILK, PLAIN OR FLAVOURED
PLENTY OF ORANGE SQUASH

*Stand an apple in
the centre of the
Cumberland sausage
ring*

Put at each place at the table a novelty for the child to take home.

After tea, give them ten minutes of Musical Bumps, a few rounds of Squeak, Piggy, Squeak, and finish with a balloon scramble while you get the Martinis ready for the mothers who come to collect.

Squeak, Piggy, Squeak is played with the children sitting round in a circle. One child is blindfolded and carries a cushion. When he has managed to find a lap, he first puts the cushion firmly on it, then sits on the cushion, saying: "Squeak, piggy, squeak." The child who is being sat on has to squeak like a pig and "he" must guess the voice. He goes round untill he identifies a voice, and then that child becomes "he."

SEVEN, EIGHT AND NINE-YEAR-OLDS

The accent here should be on competitive games of all types. The only stipulation is that there should be prizes for everyone. A dressing-up parade is always successful. So is a simple treasure hunt, a memory test and an up-to-date version of hunt-the-thimble using radar signals from outer space—"bleep-bleep" instead of the usual cold-warm-hot instructions.

For the dressing-up parade, have three grown-ups each holding a sack or pillow-case full of dressing-up bits and pieces—hats, scarves, shawls, beachwear, fans, parasols and the like. The children march round and round to music. When the music stops, the three nearest children take a piece from a sack. The adults should discreetly manoeuvre their positions to ensure equal distribution. When the sacks are empty, the children are given a few minutes to dress up. You then hold a parade before the judges and a prize is given for the best effect. It is tactful to find the runners-up so good that they must all have consolation prizes.

A treasure hunt in rhyme might test the hostess's ingenuity beforehand, but it will give her an hour of blessed peace during that nerve-racking time between tea and goodbye. Go round the house or garden a few days before, select suitable hiding places for clues and either make up or get someone to invent for you a few lines of doggerel for each clue. The more clues the merrier. (After you have made up to eight or 10 rhymes, making your own Christmas cards will be as easy as falling off a log!). Children should hunt in pairs and you should write out as many copies of each clue as there are pairs. Start them off by giving them the first clue and then stand by to see fair play. The first clue will lead them to the next, and so on. The last clue directs them to the treasure. Put the children on their honour to take only one copy of the clue from each hiding place and to keep the place a secret.

Doggerel clues

For instance, if you want them to look under the wheelbarrow, your rhyme might be:

"This may hold soil but it will not hold water.
It may belong to a son—not often a daughter
Its home is the garden, the orchard or stable.
Just push it and then find the clue (if you're able)."

This is just to give you an example. You will no doubt do much better yourself.

The menu

Anything and everything on sticks: hot sausages, kebabs, toasted cheese.

Florin-sized rolls: fill these with minced ham, chicken or salmon.

Toffee banana rolls: Sauté pieces of banana in brown sugar and butter and roll up in thin brown bread and butter.

Cracker cake: Decorate a large iced cake with miniature crackers, one for each child.

Pineapple jelly roll: Cut the lid from a large tin of pineapple rings. Pour off the juice (reserve this for fruit drink), leaving fruit in the tin. Make up a lemon or lime jelly from the instructions on the packet, but using rather less water. Fill up the tin with the jelly liquid and stand in a cold place overnight. When set, carefully cut off the end of the tin and push the jellied pineapple roll out on to a serving dish. Cut in slices between the pieces of fruit.

Coca-Cola and all kinds of fruit drink.

TEN-PLUS GROUP

These are usually quite sophisticated. They will dance the Twist, the Charleston and Eightsome reels as well as anything else up-to-date and energetic. When they get tired of that, they will grope about a darkened house very happily playing Murders and Sardines for hours.

For Murders a slip of paper for each player is put into a hat. One has "Murderer" on it and one has "Detective." The others are blank. Only the detective discloses which he has drawn. The murderer keeps his deadly secret. All players are put on their honour to speak the truth, with the exception of the murderer who can tell as many untruths as he thinks fit. Lights are extinguished all over the house and the players scatter. The murderer pounces on his victim from behind, who screams piercingly and falls to the floor. Everyone then stands stock still and the detective comes forward and assesses the situation. He then proceeds to cross-question the company until, by clever deduction, he discovers the criminal. If, after 12 questions, he cannot identify the murderer, he must make a guess. If the murderer is tracked down within that time, he must pay a forfeit. If not, he goes free.

Sardines usually ends in half-stifled hysterical laughter, but the general outline is that players scatter in a darkened house. When one bumps into another they crouch down huddled together. As each groping player stumbles upon the crouching group, he joins it, until no-one is left.

Supper menu

Children of this age will get through hundreds of hot sausages, hot dogs and an enormous bowl of hot salted fried potatoes. For some strange reason, they seem to have an insatiable appetite for prawn cocktails, as well. These are very decorative for a buffet supper table.

PRAWN COCKTAILS

Blend a little tomato purée into some well-seasoned mayonnaise. Mix into this fresh, tinned or frozen prawns or shrimps. Put shredded lettuce into the bottom of a champagne glass or goblet, add a large spoonful of the prawns or shrimps. Pipe a large rosette of seasoned whipped cream on the top, sprinkle with cayenne pepper and garnish with lemon sections.

HOT SAUSAGE DIPS

(see page 112).

HOT DOGS

(see page 52).

SAUSAGE AND MASH ROLLS

Cooked skinless sausages are covered with a thick coating of seasoned creamed potato. They are then brushed with beaten egg, rolled in crumbs and browned in hot fat. Use small paper napkins for holding.

FRESH FRUIT SALAD
COCA-COLA AND FRUIT CUP

The fruit cup should be well iced and nicely decorated (see page 59).

14: A BARBECUE

Once, when I suggested to a friend who was planning a cocktail party that she tacked a barbecue party on to the end of it, she turned pale and recoiled in horror. "I've never lit an outdoor fire in my life," she wailed piteously. "I wouldn't know how to begin."

It took me a few minutes to convince her of its absolute simplicity and the party was a roaring success. This is a splendid way of entertaining several age groups at one and the same time.

Looked at three ways . . .

There are three ways for the hostess to consider the barbecue party. Firstly, as a self-contained party, preceded only by one or two drinks. Secondly, as a way of extending a cocktail party at which snacks on a considerable scale have been served. (This means you don't need to provide massive quantities of food at the barbecue). Thirdly, as a midnight feature of an elaborate ball.

You can buy or even hire a portable barbecue set, but the home-made variety is a good substantial job and works well.

Potatoes in jackets, chicken legs, lamb cutlets, sausages and kebabs all barbecue well, as does steak. It is important to have one or two good sauces, plenty of French bread and a bowl of melted butter with which to keep the meat well basted (it is best to brush the butter on with a pastry brush). You will also need one or two long-handled forks, a good quantity of paper napkins for guests to hold the hot meats, and a container of some kind standing conveniently near to take the débris.

A barrel of beer can stand quite close to the barbecue. You can also serve bottled lager.

The table sketched (see page 99) was covered in red and white checked gingham with a square of gingham placed triangle-wise on top of it. Vine-entwined wine bottles were used as candle-holders. For other ideas on decorating tables, see page 10.

A watchman's brazier looks very inviting, and if you have a few card tables with checked cloths you will be surprised to see how delightful this all looks as the daylight fades. (See the coloured picture opposite).

The menu

Pork sausages
Potatoes
Lamb cutlets
Chicken joints
Kebabs
Piquant sauces
French bread
Toffee apples

Firm cheeses such as Cheddar, Dunlop, or Double Gloucester. (Firm cheeses should be chosen as enthusiastic guests are liable to barbecue everything within sight).
Fresh fruit
Lettuce hearts

The drinks

Pins of beer

Bottled lager

How to build a barbecue

You will need about 100 bricks and plenty of charcoal. With the bricks build two columns about 3ft high. They should be as far apart as the width of your charcoal container which rests on them.

A deep wire basket makes a good container for holding the charcoal fire. A milkman's metal bottle container, with the separating spokes removed, is ideal. Line the base with an old baking or other metal sheet and put an oven shelf on top of the bottle container to make the grid. To light your fire, you must of course remove the grid, but you can replace it when the fire is burning well. The fire will burn for as long as you need it if a bit more charcoal is added from time to time. If the container is big enough you can use half of it at a time while you stoke up the other half.

As potatoes need longer cooking than the meat, it is best to pre-cook them for an hour in a moderate oven and finish them off over the charcoal. It would not hurt to give the chicken legs a few minutes pre-cooking as well. The cutlets and sausages will take about 10 minutes on the fire, and they need to be turned a few times. They should be liberally anointed with hot butter while cooking. Sauces should be left handy.

The food

Quantities for 60 to 80 guests

20lbs large pork sausages (8 to the pound)
30lbs medium-sized potatoes, scrubbed and oiled
60 to 80 lamb cutlets (ask your butcher to trim and point these for you)
60 to 80 chicken joints
60 to 80 kebabs (a small bacon roll, a cocktail sausage, a piece of mushroom and a small piece of lamb or beef, are threaded on to a metal skewer)
16 to 24 sticks of French bread
3lbs butter for basting
2 to 3doz toffee apples
10lbs cheeses
1 firkin and 1 pin of beer (a firkin is 72pts, a pin 36pts: your local landlord will supply and tap these for you)
1 case of lager (at least)
Large basket fresh fruit
Large bowl lettuce hearts

A good working lay-out for your barbecue

These quantities presuppose that your guests have not had large snacks with their cocktails. If they have, you may halve the number of sausages, potatoes and French loaves.

TOFFEE APPLES

INGREDIENTS: 1½lbs brown sugar; ½pt water; 12oz golden syrup; a good pinch of cream of tartar; 6oz butter; 20 apples.

METHOD: Put the sugar and water into a pan over low heat until sugar is dissolved. Add syrup, cream of tartar and butter. Bring to the boil and heat to 270 deg. F. To test, drop a little in cold water: it will set if cooked.

Impale each apple on a wooden skewer and dip into the toffee. Stand on greased paper until almost set and then dip a second time.

The sauces

PEPPER SHERRY

Fill a bottle half full with small red chillies and top up with sherry: cork tightly. This will keep, and you can add more sherry from time to time. Use a sprinkler top for this sauce, as it is very hot and only a few drops are necessary.

BARBECUE SAUCE

INGREDIENTS: 12 large minced onions; 1lb butter; 3 cups tomato ketch-up; ½ cup lemon juice; ½ cup vinegar; ¾lb brown sugar; 12 teaspoonsful prepared mustard; 12 tablespoonsful Worcester sauce; 1 tablespoonful salt.

METHOD: Sauté onion in the butter; add remaining ingredients and simmer until onion is cooked.

15: GARAGE PARTY FOR TEENAGERS

Experienced party-givers will know that nothing sets party spirits soaring so adequately as a pleasing and unusual background. Each season sees frenzied attempts to acquire that elusive "something" which a successful décor provides and the lack of which can ruin a party within the first few minutes.

Expense often has little to do with creating a successful atmosphere—ingenuity and imagination everything.

The teenage party has more potentiality than any other as it lends itself readily to unusual treatment, so let us "blueprint" one which, although not ruinous in price, will have a rich and rare personality.

The first thing is to forget about the drawing-room. A good, long look at spare rooms, attics, cellars, stables or barns is indicated here. Even a backyard or garage is not to be despised.

The disguise

The party setting described in this chapter was done in a small garage measuring approximately 20ft by 10ft, which will accommodate 20 to 30 young people. It was dressed almost entirely in crêpe paper—36 rolls, costing 6d per roll.

After emptying the garage completely the first step is to examine the floor. If this is even and in good condition a thorough scrubbing and a good application of French chalk will make a passable floor for dancing.

The walls will need a disguise, so make a frame on which to hang drapes of the crêpe paper. Laths of wood should be nailed all round the top where the walls and ceiling join and also at the bottom of the walls just above the floor level.

These laths can be bought at timber merchants' for a few shillings a bundle. The garage is now ready for the exciting part of the treatment.

The colour scheme used in the garage seen in the sketch on the next page was candy-striped walls in white and shocking pink with narrower panels in a deeper pink to hide the joins, and a midnight-blue ceiling. The ceiling was put into position first.

Lengths of black twine were attached to the laths on the back wall every 12in and stretched forward and fastened firmly on to the lath over the doors.

This twine made an invisible support for the lengths of midnight-blue paper which were placed above it running from side to side, the ends being drawing-pinned to the laths at the top of the side walls.

Next the alternating stripes of pink and white for the walls were pinned into place, then the narrow deep-pink panels placed over the joins. (When using crêpe paper always stretch it well to ensure a good, taut fit.) A swagged pelmet was then fixed at the top of the wall panels running all the way round and a straight piece of the crêpe at the bottom made a skirting board.

The garage doors were an important feature. They were covered with imitation stone wallpaper (it took two pieces at 7s a piece) and then decorated with wooden garden trellis-work into which were twined long strands of greenery and bunches of oranges and lemons.

Coloured spotlights were fixed in the two back corners.

Now for the food

Once the garage was decorated for the party there came the question of the table (see page 10) and—more important—what to put on it in the way of party food. There are half a dozen perennial favourites in party menus for the young. They like hot dogs, Swiss fondue, fresh fruit, an assortment of continental sausage, pilaf or risotto, a robust sandwich like the Niçoise Pan Bagnat, and something like an English version of a cassoulet or the American pork 'n' beans.

For the hot dogs have bridge rolls and a large pot of French mustard beside a small table heater holding a casserole dish full of boiling Frankfurter sausages. Guests can then make their own.

The Swiss fondue can also be put on to a table heater (or it can be made in a dish with its own little burner under it). A toasted loaf accompanies this for dunking. Use a long tea loaf with all crusts removed except the bottom one, then cut twice lengthwise to within an inch of the bottom crust and then across in 1in slices.

The whole is then brushed over with melted butter and baked until golden brown and crisp. This is then stood on a tray with the bubbling fondue. Use fingers or forks for dunking the toasted bread. The art is to remove it without loss and eat it without scalding your mouth.

The fresh fruit is piled on to a platter and two or three varieties of cheese added. The continental sausage can be cut into slices and served on sticks together with chunks of hot French bread. The cassoulet is carried to the table in something like a Lancashire hot-pot dish.

Cassoulet is a splendid and satisfying dish and, although few can aspire to the preserved goose which is part of the classic French recipe, a very satisfactory compromise can be made between this and the American version.

CASSOULET

INGREDIENTS: 3lbs white haricot beans; 2lbs belly of pork; a medium sized leg of lamb; 2lbs fresh garlic sausage; 2lbs smoked gammon; 6 cloves of garlic; bouquet garni (bay leaf, thyme and parsley); 6oz lard; 2 onions; seasoning; fresh breadcrumbs. These quantities are sufficient for 20.

METHOD: Soak the beans and gammon overnight. Then put them in a large casserole, chop the onions and garlic and add with the garlic sausage (de-rinded if necessary) and bouquet garni. Cover with fresh water and cook in a slow oven for four hours.

Meanwhile roast the pork and lamb in the lard. When cooked, remove all meat from the bone of the leg of lamb. When the beans are practically cooked, take out the piece of gammon and cut it and all meats and sausage into convenient pieces.

Put meat and beans in alternate layers in a large hot-pot dish or other deep earthenware pot. Sprinkle layers with pepper and a little salt if needed. Barely cover with the liquid in which the beans have been cooking. Sprinkle a thick layer of breadcrumbs on the top and return to a slow oven to finish cooking. A further half hour should suffice. The cassoulet is ready when a golden brown crust has formed.

PAN BAGNAT
(Niçoise salad filling)

A Pan Bagnat is a complete Niçoise salad filling placed between the two halves of a North Country tea cake or Scottish bap. Long pieces of crusty French bread sliced in half lengthwise may also be used.

The filling for each one: 2 or 3 shredded lettuce leaves; 1 large tomato, sliced; 1 sliced hard-boiled egg; 6 small black olives; 2 or 3 sliced radishes; 1 chopped slice cucumber; 4 anchovy fillets; a little thinly-sliced green pepper; chopped thin slice onion; 1 tablespoonful tuna fish.

METHOD: Cut the bread in half lengthwise and place the shredded lettuce on the bottom half and the rest of the salad on the lettuce. The classic French recipe calls for the bread to be previously soaked in the oil from the anchovies but this is sometimes unpalatable for English taste. A better way is to dress with a good garlic dressing just before it is needed.

SWISS FONDUE

For the recipe see page 112.

Now for the drinks

A good cup or a few bottles of a sparkling Anjou (very sophisticated and smart, the latter) or they would like, no doubt, a refreshing summer drink which the market people drink in Monaco. This is called a Monégasque and is a mixture of half well-chilled white wine and half bottled lemonade.

16: A CHRISTENING PARTY

This is usually a simple, homely party for guests of all age groups. With the very old and very young in mind, there has been a move recently to replace the traditional rich fruit Christening cake by a much less elaborate one—very often a sponge layer cake. This is still iced and decorated in the usual way, except that no almond paste is used.

This type of cake can be served in larger slices than the usual fingers of rich cake and generally pleases everyone.

If the Christening ceremony takes place in the morning, a pre-lunch party on the lines of a cocktail party is usually given (see page 27). If in the afternoon, a tea party fills the bill nicely. In either case, however, a glass of champagne or sparkling wine is almost an essential with which to drink the toast to the most important, but usually highly indifferent and unconcerned, member of the party.

The setting

A doting godmother might like to create the party setting. She should make the buffet table look dainty and frilly. White lace or nylon flock makes a very attractive floor-reaching flounce for the front of the table. The cake can either be the centrepiece or can have its own little table. Whichever is decided, decorate the cake with a wide satin ribbon and fresh flowers. Small posies of the same kind of flowers can also be dotted about on the table or used to garnish the platters of food.

AFTERNOON CHRISTENING PARTY
FOR 30

The menu

60 savoury éclairs
60 salmon and cucumber circles (see page 112 substituting salmon for prawns)
60 to 90 chicken rolls (see tiny hamburgers page 120)
60 small assorted sandwiches
40 small Eccles cakes

40 small meringues
40 frosted lemon cakes
Christening cake
Indian and China tea
Champagne or sparkling wine
Home-made ginger beer for the children

The recipes

SAVOURY ECLAIRS

Unsweetened choux paste* is piped into small fingers and baked at Gas Reg. No. 6 (403 deg. F.) for 30 mins. These can then be split and filled with any savoury filling. For example, minced ham with mango chutney, minced chicken with a little mayonnaise, chopped prawns or shrimps mixed with creamed butter to which a few drops of lemon juice have been added, or mushroom butter (see page 60). Brush the éclairs with aspic on the point of setting and sprinkle with minced radishes.

*CHOUX PASTE

INGREDIENTS: ½lb plain flour; 6oz butter; ¾pt water; 6 eggs; a good pinch of salt.

METHOD: Sieve the flour, then boil the butter, water and salt in a saucepan. Remove from the heat and beat in the flour a little at a time. Allow to cool then add the beaten eggs a little at a time. Continue beating until smooth.

ECCLES CAKES

Cut out 3in circles of thinly rolled puff pastry. In the centres put spoonsful of cleaned currants mixed with melted butter and brown sugar. Shape into rounds by pinching edges to centre, put on to a baking sheet with the joined edges underneath, flatten slightly and prick them all over. Brush with beaten egg and bake at Gas Reg. No. 7 (424 deg. F.) for 10 mins. Dust with icing sugar. To make 40 you will need 2½lbs puff pastry and ¾lb of currant mixture.

SMALL MERINGUES

INGREDIENTS to make 40: 8 egg-whites; 1lb castor sugar; pinch of salt.

METHOD: Whisk egg-whites and salt together until quite stiff. Add 1oz of the sugar and continue to whisk until very dry. Fold in the remainder of the sugar lightly. Pipe the mixture on to oiled trays with a large rose pipe. Bake at Gas Reg. No. ¼ (200 deg. F.) for about 1½ hours or until set and dry.

CHRISTENING CAKE
(Sponge layer cake)

For this number two sandwich cakes should be baked in 12in sandwich-cake tins. 1lb each of flour, butter and sugar, and eight eggs is sufficient for these two cakes. For recipe see Easter Bunny cake on page 88.

FIZZY GINGER BEER
(an alternative to champagne for the children)

INGREDIENTS: 8 lemons; 1½lbs sugar; 1½oz whole ginger (bruised); ½oz cream of tartar; 1oz yeast; 10pts boiling water.

METHOD: Peel the lemons and cut them into thin slices. Remove the pips. Put the slices and the peel into an earthenware bowl with the sugar, ginger, and cream of tartar. Pour over the boiling water and allow to stand until lukewarm then crumble the yeast into the bowl. Stand in a warm place for 24 hours then skim and strain into bottles. Tie the corks securely. This is ready for drinking in two to three days.

Sandwich making

Use quartern loaves specially ordered from your baker. Place the loaf lengthwise on the table. Cut off every crust except the bottom one and the left-hand side one. If you are left-handed, leave the right-hand crust on. It is to enable you to hold the loaf firmly with the flat of your hand.

Slice the loaf lengthwise across the top, holding the loaf firm against the side crust. When you have filled and sandwiched the slices together (see below for fillings) trim the edges and cut into whatever shapes you wish. Out of a double slice you will get 16 2½in circular sandwiches, or you can use a 5in circular cutter and cut them in half again to make a crescent.

Sandwich fillings

Minced ham bound with mustard and mixed with chopped hard-boiled egg

Creamed butter and sieved sardine mixed together. Put slices of hard-boiled eggs on top of this

Crab-meat, seasoned with salt, pepper and lemon juice, mixed with coarsely-chopped lettuce leaves.

Green peppers with chopped hard-boiled eggs and a few chopped chives.

Minced chicken with horseradish cream.

Chopped nuts and minced candied peel.

17: THE NIGHT WHEN
WITCHES FLY LOW

The origin of Hallowe'en, half pagan, half Christian, is almost lost in time, although some of its customary rites linger on. There is no doubt that the night when witches ride the wild sky and lost souls come home for comfort is the night for candlelight, a blazing log fire and the first of the "cosy" parties of winter.

Spooky lights

The setting for this party should be mostly traditional. The first essential is a "spooky" dimly-lit room. To make the lights, choose large round, uncooked pumpkins, turnips or beetroots. Cut a slice from the top of each, and, with a spoon, scoop out most of the pulp. Using a very sharp pointed knife, cut holes in the skin to represent eyes, nose and mouth. Melt the bottom of a small candle and fix it firmly inside the lantern, sticking it on to the base with the melted wax. Make a hole on each side at the top and put a wire through for hanging.

Black cats and broomsticks

An indoor room needs a bit of treatment to get the right atmosphere. Black material or paper should be hung on to the walls and cut-outs of black cats, owls, skulls and cross-bones, demons and such-like pasted on. Crossed broomsticks could be hung on the walls, too.

Small tables could be covered with cloths of red and black, and each table should be lit by a small turnip or beetroot lantern.

Witches' cauldron
for soup or punch

In the darkest corner is the witches' cauldron. This can hold either soup or good strong punch. Any old cauldron-shaped cooking pot suspended from a handle is suitable—even if, in the interests of hygiene, it has another container inside it. In this case, the cauldron could have a little boiling water in it to keep the contents of the inner container hot.

To be really effective, the cauldron should swing from a tripod. Failing this, it could hang from a hook screwed under the mantelpiece.

Buffet table in black

If your party room is big enough, put up a trestle table or something similar and use it as a buffet table. You could cover this with black material and stick on crescent moons and stars cut from kitchen foil.

The food
This should be seasonal. In addition to the buffet, have chestnuts roasting (a jumping nut means a faithless lover, a quiet nut a faithful one).

The menu for 25 guests
Leek and potato soup
Devilled chicken
Pork baked in apples

Jacket potatoes
Casserole jardinière
Pumpkin pie and Hot punch

The recipes

DEVILLED CHICKEN
INGREDIENTS: 40 to 50 joints of chicken; butter for basting; curry powder; chutney.

METHOD: Partly roast the chicken joints in the butter. Remove from the oven and score deeply with a sharp knife. Sprinkle with curry powder and then roll them in the chutney, pressing the chutney well into the cuts. Return them to oven until cooked. Baste frequently. Serve hot or cold.

PORK BAKED IN APPLES
INGREDIENTS: 25 large cooking apples; ½lb butter; 20 shallots or 10 medium-sized onions; 2lbs pork; 6 cloves garlic; 3 tablespoonsful made English mustard; 3 tablespoonsful soya sauce; ½lb seedless raisins; juice of 3 lemons; 1lb demerara sugar; 6 tablespoonsful chunky marmalade; salt and pepper; bottle of white wine. For the garnish: sweet corn kernels; bacon rolls.

METHOD: Core the apples and scoop out sufficient pulp to make a good cavity. Melt the butter in a heavy pan, add the shallots or onions, chopped finely, and cook for a few minutes. Cut the pork into 1in cubes and add. Cook together for 5 mins over a gentle heat. Add the crushed garlic, mustard, soya sauce, raisins, lemon juice and sugar.

Chop the marmalade peel into small pieces and add it to the pan. Season. Add a little of the wine and cook gently for 30 to 40 mins, adding more wine from time to time. When cooked, stuff the apples with the mixture, stand them in a baking tin with a little water, cover with foil and bake at Gas Reg. No. 4 (358 deg. F.) for about 20 mins, but the cooking time entirely depends on the type of apple. They should be just cooked through, but not allowed to fall away. These may be served on a bed of sweet corn kernels and garnished with bacon rolls.

CASSEROLE JARDINIERE

INGREDIENTS: 4oz butter; 12 shallots or 4 large onions; 4 medium-sized marrows; 4 cucumbers; salt and pepper; 4 cloves garlic; bouquet garni (thyme, parsley, bayleaf); 4lbs green tomatoes; white breadcrumbs.

METHOD: Melt butter in a thick-bottomed pan. Add finely-chopped shallots or onions and cook gently for a few minutes without browning. Peel and de-seed marrows and cucumbers, cut them into cubes and add, with the seasoning, garlic and bouquet garni. Cook gently for 15 mins, stirring well. Skin tomatoes by making a cut all the way round and then putting them into boiling water for a minute or so. Cut them into sections and add to the pan. Cook altogether for a further 15 to 20 mins or until green tomatoes are cooked. If there is too much liquid, reduce by very rapid boiling, but stir again to avoid burning. Remove bouquet garni, correct seasoning, pour into an ovenproof dish, scatter breadcrumbs on the top and cook in a moderate oven until brown.

PUMPKIN PIE

INGREDIENTS: 2lbs sweet pastry; 1 pumpkin; 1½lbs brown sugar; 8 eggs; 2 tablespoonsful chopped crystallized orange peel; 1 tablespoonful cinnamon; juice of 3 lemons; ½pt thick cream, whipped.

METHOD: Line 1 very large or 4 small pie-tins with the pastry. Prick and bake. Meanwhile peel and seed quite a large pumpkin, and put it into a pan with the sugar and a little water. Cook until tender. Allow to cool, then put through a sieve. Separate eggs, beat yolks and add, with the orange peel, cinnamon, and lemon juice, to the pumpkin. Fold in whipped egg-whites and whipped cream. Fill pie case(s) with mixture and bake at Gas Reg. No. 5 (379 deg. F.) for 30 to 40 mins.

HOT PUNCH

INGREDIENTS: rum; pineapple juice; lemon juice; bar syrup (see page 59); Angostura bitters; garnish of lemon and apple slices.

METHOD: For 25 drinks, to one bottle of rum you will need one tin of pineapple juice, and the juice of 4 lemons. Put juices into a pan with twice the amount of water. Add bar syrup to taste. Bring to the boil and add rum when you are ready to serve it. Then add a very few drops (and I mean this) of Angostura bitters. Float lemon and apple slices on top.

18: A COMING OF AGE

Most 21-year-olds scorn the idea of a strictly formal coming of age celebration, yet when it is pointed out to them that parents, godparents and
grandparents expect to be fitted in to the party picture they are at a loss.
A compromise is the answer, a party with two distinct flavours—a hint of
white-glove formality for the older guests and an off-beat touch for the
young ones.

This can be a highly successful please-everybody evening, but there are
two essentials. One is a comfortable sitting-room for the older guests
—"The Dowagers' Room." The other is a completely separate feature
with a distinctly youthful personality. It can be beatnik, barbecue, bistro
or night club. This is for the young and it should be understood that there
must be no trespassing.

Here we plan a party for 40 young and 20 older guests. It is run in three
stages, starting with a cocktail party.

1 THE COCKTAIL PARTY FOR EVERYONE: The first part of the evening is
run as a cocktail party, all age groups together, the birthday child receiving congratulations and the cake-cutting and toasts, if any, disposed of.
Later, prompted by parents, the party begins to operate on two levels.

2 FOR THE OLDER GUESTS: Older guests should then be comfortably
settled in the "Dowagers' Room" with an adequate supply of short drinks
and perhaps a bridge table or two.

3 FOR THE YOUNG: The young ones now take over their particular setting. This can be an attic, cellar, spare room, kitchen, stable, garage or terrace. It can be decorated in many ways.

THE COCKTAIL PARTY FOR 60 GUESTS

Use the largest room for this section of the party. It may be necessary
to move out some of the furniture. Almost certainly it will be essential to
have the bar and buffet in the room as the kitchen will have to be kept as
clear as possible for the preparation of food to be served later in the
evening. No drinks should come from the kitchen, then, so the bar should
be well-planned and self-supporting.

The setting

The setting in the cocktail party room should be smart and formal to
contrast with the gay and casual atmosphere of the feature for the younger
guests.

The food

There should be attractive platters of small savouries and one or two interesting "dips," but this menu need not be over-lavish as later in the evening there will be more substantial food (barbecue food or sausage and mash type for the younger guests, one or two more sophisticated dishes for the older guests).

It is obvious that with a party of this type a certain amount of help will be needed in the kitchen. The cocktail party food could be prepared beforehand, as could the big dish which is to be served later to the older guests, but the timing will be difficult unless there is someone to re-fill platters, heat up the main dish if necessary and make the coffee.

The menu

120 small savoury patties
120 prawn and cucumber circles
3 quartern loaves made into roly-poly sandwiches (about 250 small whirls)
3 tins Swiss fondue
3 French or toasted loaves for dunking

Sausage dip using
6lbs chipolata sausages, 16 to the pound, each one twisted in two. Prevent bursting by placing sausage strings in wire basket; lower into barely melted oil or lard. Bring slowly to near boiling heat. Cook for about 20 mins.
60 assorted cheese savouries

For other cocktail party food, see page 30.

The drinks

In addition to the usual short drinks for the cocktail party, it would be a good idea to include some wine—red, white and rosé.

A pleasant and refreshing summer drink with wine as a base is a Moselle Kalte Ente, or "Cold Duck." This is made by pouring two bottles of chilled Moselle wine, one still, one sparkling, into a tall chilled jug which has a spiral of lemon peel attached to the rim. Both bottles are poured at the same time, one in either hand.

There should always be one non-alcoholic drink. A mixture of melon, syrup, orange-flower water and soda water well iced is fragrant and delicious (see page 116). If you care to drink champagne or other sparkling wine during the evening, perhaps for the toasts, see that it is well chilled. See page 54 for advice on opening and pouring.

The recipes

ROLY-POLY SANDWICHES

For instructions on making these, see page 89. Fillings can be smoked salmon, smoked cod's roe, minced ham mixed with a good mustard sauce (see page 112), blue cheese mixed up with butter and a little horseradish, or Brie mixed with Dutch cheese, port wine and some chopped celery.

PRAWN AND CUCUMBER CIRCLES

Cut circles of white or brown bread with a 2in cutter. Spread liberally with butter. Cut small circles from the middle of slices of cucumber and put the outer circles on the buttered bread. Fill the cavities with one or two prawns each, spoon a little mayonnaise over them and sprinkle with paprika.

SMALL SAVOURY PATTIES

Small circles of puff pastry are cut with a 2in cutter, brushed with beaten egg, baked in a hot oven and then split and filled with any of the following combined with a little Béchamel sauce: cooked mushroom, cheese, lobster, crab, chicken, curried beef, or a mixture of cheese, onion and tomato cooked together.

SWISS FONDUE

It is much less trouble to buy this ready-made in tins, but, should you wish to make it, here is a recipe from the Jura. Put into a very heavy saucepan 4 crushed cloves of garlic, 4 glasses of dry white wine and 2lbs of Gruyère cheese cut into small pieces. Stir continuously until the cheese has melted. Add a little Kirsch, season well and keep hot. *To make a toasted loaf for dunking,* use a half-quartern loaf. Remove all the crusts except the bottom one. Use a sharp knife and make eight or nine cuts across the loaf, cutting right down to within an inch of the bottom crust. Then turn a narrow side of the loaf towards you and make three long cuts almost down to the bottom crust. You will have made from 24 to 27 cubed fingers which are still attached to the loaf. Brush the whole thing with melted butter and put it into the oven at Gas Reg. No. 4 (358 deg. F.), and bake until it is golden-brown. You must put the loaf on its side while it is baking and if you can arrange it into an arched semi-circle and keep all the cubes an even distance from each other by wedging with small pieces of crust, when it is baked you will have a firm arch of golden fingers which will stand up like a suspension bridge. Guests pull the fingers of toast from the "bridge" themselves and dunk them into the hot cheese. If you have an earthenware skillet or casserole which fits over a small spirit lamp you will be able to keep the cheese bubbling away until it is all eaten.

SAUSAGE DIP

For the "dip" use a large Coburg or cottage loaf. Cut the crust off very thinly, leaving only the bottom crust. Cut a small slice from the top and scoop out a piece from the centre of the loaf to make a "well" to hold mustard sauce*. Brush over with beaten egg and bake in the oven until golden-brown. When ready to serve, fill with sauce, put the cooked sausages (see page 52 for cooking instructions) on cocktail sticks and spike all round the loaf.

*MUSTARD SAUCE: Mix the contents of two jars of French mustard with tarragon vinegar, 2oz of castor sugar and a few drops of Worcester sauce. Mix in a little made English mustard and a tablespoonful of olive oil.

ASSORTED CHEESE SAVOURIES
Beat a little horseradish sauce into some soft cream cheese. Add a little sugar, salt and pepper. Mince a handful of fresh radishes quite finely. Make little round pellets with the cheese mixture and roll them in the minced radish. Top each with half of a de-seeded black or green grape, put cocktail sticks right through and serve in small sweet cases. To vary these, cherries may be used or the cheese shaped into small rolls with a piece of pineapple inside.

The equipment
(See page 116)

SUPPER FOR 20 OLDER GUESTS

A whole garnished salmon with salad (see page 24) would be fine as it could be prepared well in advance. Honeytang chicken, a ham mousse, or a chicken salad (see page 17) would all be very suitable and enjoyable for the older guests.

This main dish would be served much later in the evening. It could be put on the table you have used for the cocktail party bar. Beside the dish place a pile of plates, forks and paper napkins. Guests will help themselves. A large tray of coffee could also be brought in here, guests pouring for themselves. Choose a main dish from the following list:

The menu
A whole garnished salmon   *Ham mousse*
Honeytang chicken   *Fruits de mer cocktail*

The drinks
(see page 116)

The recipes
HONEYTANG CHICKEN
INGREDIENTS: 6 3-4lb broiler chickens; 4 jars of French mustard; 4 1lb jars of honey; 8oz curry powder; clove of garlic; 6 bananas; little brown sugar; rice; ½lb butter; 1 glass red wine.

METHOD: Make a cream with the butter and work half of the curry powder into it. Spread this over the birds and put them in the oven to roast for an hour. Baste frequently. Meanwhile make the honeytang sauce. Use a thick saucepan and melt the honey; add the juice of the garlic, the French mustard and the rest of the curry powder worked to a smooth paste with the wine. Simmer gently for 30 mins. Joint the cooked birds and remove all bones. Put into the saucepan with the sauce and cook together very gently for a few minutes. Stir to prevent sticking. Cut the bananas into quarters and sauté them in the liquid in the roasting-tin, having previously sprinkled them with brown sugar. To serve the chicken, put the joints on a platter, surround them with a border of cooked rice and garnish with the bananas.

AN EASY WAY TO COOK RICE

Use long-grained rice and for each cupful allow exactly two cups of white stock or water. Fry a very finely-chopped onion in a little oil. Add the dry rice and turn several times until it is well coated with the oil. Add the liquid and bring to the boil. Put a buttered paper over the rice, place a close-fitting lid over the pan and put it into the oven at Gas Reg. No. 5 (397 deg. F.) for 20 mins. It is now ready to use.

HAM MOUSSE

INGREDIENTS: 4lbs ham; 8 egg-whites; 2pts thick cream; 4 tablespoons-ful tomato purée; 4oz aspic crystals; seasoning; 1pt of mayonnaise.

METHOD: Mince and pound the ham as smooth as possible, then stir in the tomato purée. Stir the mayonnaise into the ham mixture. Season. Melt the aspic crystals in a little hot water, allow to cool and then add to the mixture a little at a time. Partly whip the cream—it should thicken but still be very light. Fold it into the mixture. Lastly fold in the whipped egg-whites. Pour into greased moulds or soufflé dishes. If the latter, turn out when set and decorate with spears of chicory all round as in a charlotte russe (see page 19). If moulds are used, turn out, pipe with a little sea-soned cream and garnish with minced radishes and chopped parsley.

FRUITS DE MER COCKTAIL

INGREDIENTS: 2 large packs of scampi; 2 lobsters or 2 tins of lobster; 1 large pack of shrimps; 2 quarts fresh mussels or 4 jars of ready-cooked; 1½pts mayonnaise (see page 41); a little tomato purée; 1 cup of whipped cream; seasoning; shredded lettuce.

METHOD: Clean and cook the mussels* (these are not everyone's fav-ourite but delicious). Cook the scampi and add both to the shrimps and cut-up lobster meat in a large mixing-bowl. Mix together and season. Combine the tomato purée with the mayonnaise and bind the shellfish with half of it. Pile up on to an oval-shaped platter. Fold the whipped cream into the rest of the mayonnaise and spoon over the fish. Surround with a border of shredded lettuce dotted with "riders" of lemon. Serve with little de-crusted rolls (see below) of thin brown bread and butter.

*TO COOK MUSSELS: The shells of the mussels should be scraped and the beards removed. They should then be put into clean cold water and given a thorough moving about to remove all grit and sand. Do this several times. They should then be cooked in seasoned water to which has been added some onion, parsley and thyme, for three to four minutes, or until the shells open. When cooked, remove from the shell and use as required.

TO MAKE ROLLS OF BREAD AND BUTTER: Cut lengthwise slices from a large brown loaf. Spread with butter. De-crust and cut each piece into four. Roll up neatly like a Swiss roll.

The equipment
(See page 116).

FOOD FOR 40 YOUNG GUESTS
THE BARBECUE

If the young have voted for a barbecue as their special feature, this should be built earlier in the day (see page 98). The food should be set out on trays, ready to be taken out as needed. The sauces, French bread, butter for basting, paper napkins for holding the hot meats and so on, should all be assembled.

A large, non-clinical kitchen (not many about, alas) is perfect for a beer and sausage party (see page 49) with a white scrubbed kitchen table for the buffet, strings of onions, bunches of herbs and a big trug full of fruits and vegetables as decoration.

THE KITCHEN PARTY

The menu

Platters of English and Continental sausages
Large dish of sausage and mash
Large open sandwiches of French bread with ham, beef, tongue, *or chicken, liberally garnished with sliced tomato, cucumber, lettuce, watercress, olives, radishes, and mayonnaise*

The drinks
Serve beer (see page 116 for quantities).

The equipment
(see page 116).

THE NIGHT-CLUB PARTY

For advice on this "breakfast" type food see page 117. If instead of a barbecue or kitchen party they plan the separate feature on night club lines, the supper food needs to be slightly "smarter". An attic or cellar is the ideal setting, very dimly lit. Hang walls with dark red paper and do the ceiling in black (see page 100). Have small circular tables with red sateen or felt cloths and place runners of black and white striped mattress ticking on top.

The menu
Bacon and eggs
Kedgeree
Scrambled eggs with Frankfurter sausages

The drinks
Serve beer (see page 116 for quantities).

The recipe

KEDGEREE

INGREDIENTS: 3lbs cooked rice; 3lbs cooked smoked haddock; 1lb butter; 1pt cream; 12 hard-boiled eggs; seasoning.

METHOD: Heat the butter in a thick saucepan and add the fish and chopped hard-boiled eggs. Stir until very hot and then add the rice, a little at a time, seasoning as you go. When it is all combined and very hot, add the cream and cook a little longer. Serve very hot sprinkled with chopped parsley.

Quantities of drink for all three parties (60 guests)

36 bottles of wine, including some sparkling Moselle
2 pins of beer (for barbecue, kitchen or night-club party)
8 bottles of whisky
8 bottles of gin
2 bottles of medium dry sherry
6 syphons of soda water

36 "splits" of bitter lemon
36 "splits" of tonic water
36 "splits" of ginger ale
1 gallon of Melonade (see below)
12 bottles of champagne or other sparkling wine (this will allow 1 glass each for the toasts). More of this if you wish.

MELONADE

Rub 1lb ripe melon pulp through a sieve (the flesh of about 2 large melons). Pour over it 1pt boiling bar syrup (see page 59). Stand until cold. (Make this drink several hours before it is needed). Strain and add 2 tablespoonsful of orange-flower water. Put on ice until it is very cold. Dilute to taste with soda water.

This drink looks very attractive if some balls of melon are cut out with a vegetable scoop and added to the jug or glasses. It should also contain a few segments of orange.

Equipment necessary for all three parties

120 8oz Paris goblets
24 sherry glasses
40 beer mugs
2 large trays for drinks
3 large glass jugs
48 small plates
24 large plates
40 knives
60 forks
Large serving spoons and forks
12 ashtrays
300 paper napkins (most of these

would be for the barbecue)
Dishes and platters for cocktail food
Meat trays and bowls for the barbecue table
Pastry brush for basting with melted butter
2 long-handled forks
20 or so coffee cups, saucers and spoons
2 large coffee pots
2 cream jugs and sugar basins

19: A DANCE IN THE HOME

The idea of a dance at home may seem a bit overwhelming at first. One compares it instinctively with the grand type of coming-out dance whose pattern does not change very much from season to season. Its formula is more or less as it was in the beginning, is now and ever shall be, with the tiaras, the top bands, the kedgeree, champagne and preceding dinner parties. These are all part of a time-honoured ritual and a less ambitious effort may appear very homespun indeed.

But this need not be the case. It is quite possible to adapt the "grand manner" routine to an inexpensive miniature version of the more lavish affair.

A 10 p.m. start

A society dance starts at 10 p.m. or thereabouts. There is something sumptuous about this late start and it also has the merit of providing time for leisurely preparation after a day's work.

It is reasonable to suppose that most people will have had something to eat so that a lavish supper buffet is not essential. Attractive finger food with a few interesting novelties is all that is necessary at this stage. This buffet runs from 10 p.m. onwards.

A 2 a.m. breakfast

What is very, very important is to have a really splendid breakfast: this will raise the status of your dance more than anything. Bacon and eggs, scrambled eggs, sausages, kidneys and mushrooms, served at 2 a.m., will give your party a lift out of all proportion to the modest cost involved. But adequate seating accommodation is essential so that breakfast may be eaten in comfort. You must have good help in the kitchen to ensure that the breakfast is served freshly cooked.

Quick service

A certain amount of preparation will ensure that the food to be cooked is ready for quick service. For instance, eggs to be scrambled can be beaten up, seasoned and put into a large bowl sitting on top of a pan of boiling water (eggs cooked in this way can be left for a long time to look after themselves — they only need an occasional stir). Bacon can be bought de-rinded and can be cooked in the oven, as can sausages and mushrooms. Kidneys can be cooked beforehand and heated up when needed. This leaves frying the eggs as the only immediate job. With two clean frying pans, some lard and a couple of fish slicers, this can be done quite expertly, even for 40 people.

Another pair of hands is needed to dish up all this delectable food on to platters. These can then be placed piping hot on to the buffet table, so that the guests can help themselves. There will need to be several large platters, and second helpings should be allowed for. Coffee should be made beforehand and kept hot.

The setting

If the dance is to be in the house, let the state of the floor decide which room is to be the ballroom, then you will need a separate room to hold your buffet table from which the finger food and breakfast food will be served.

In the room chosen for dancing, the carpets should come up and if the floor is in reasonable condition an application of polish and plenty of elbow-grease will make quite a passable dance floor. If it is really bad, you might consider hiring for one day a re-surfacing machine; you can get this from a local firm specialising in cleaning or even from a good builder.

These large industrial machines are very efficient and will whip up a good surface in no time. If you can run to a marquee the whole operation can take place under one roof. The tent people can lay an excellent dance floor.

Unless it is intended to present the dance room in a completely new light, using bunting or strong crêpe paper to disguise the walls (see page 100) there need be very little done with the exception of large flower arrangements well up on high mantelpieces or pedestals and softening lights by replacing existing light bulbs with pink ones.

Cut a dash

You can, however, cut a dash with your buffet room. Here the setting can either be formal, with the buffet table dressed with a pleated satin flounce to match existing furnishings or a particularly striking idea would be a red sateen or felt covering for your buffet table with large black or white motifs appliquéd on to it.

There would need to be small tables and these could have floor-reaching black or red cloths. Small arrangements of gilded fruits (use a gold paint spray for this) on each table could hold tall red or black candles. Alternatively, a black and white décor could be highlighted by a black-painted trug holding an arrangement of silvered gourds and cobs of corn.

If you are using a marquee, you must take the colour of the lining into consideration and dress your buffet table and small tables accordingly. (For petticoated tables, see page 13).

Choose the band with care

Any young person will tell you that however good the setting, however sumptuous the food, a dance is a flop if the band is not good. Take a bit of trouble over this important item. There are some very good amateur bands available and your young people may know of one. Any association for boys would be worth trying for a reasonable band; a students' hostel is also a good bet. Failing that, there are agents in almost every town who will put you in touch with a suitable one. If the cost is beyond your reach, there are still ways and means. One of the most successful small home dances I have ever known had a really good programme of music from all the well-known bands which had been carefully chosen from currently-popular records. Or you can now hire a juke-box.

Welcome with a drink

Upon arrival, guests should be handed a drink. It can either be sherry, a straightforward gin or whisky, a "cup", a Pimmlet (see page 121), a sparkling wine, a chilled rosé or white wine or, of course, champagne. And the music should start immediately before the arrival of the first guest. The combination of a good drink and a good tune will quickly get this party off on the right foot.

Finger food at the ready

At this stage the buffet table is already laid with the finger food. Later the platters of hot breakfast food are brought in. Breakfast menus should be put on the small tables which are already laid, buffet-style, with knives, forks and paper napkins. The drink now is lager or light ale.

The bar

Don't mix up the food and drink. Have a separate bar if possible. If there is no third room in the house, the widest part of the hall could be used, a narrow 4ft to 6ft table being ample. The nearer to the kitchen this is, the better, to facilitate fresh supplies of chilled drinks and clean glasses. The breakfast beer can also be served from here.

The cloakroom and powder-room

If you have a daily woman this is where you bring her into the picture. She can show guests up to a room which has been set aside as a cloakroom and powder-room.

Cloakroom tickets are not really necessary, but it might be useful to have an extra table to put coats across. A supply of face tissues, frozen cologne and aspirin will be appreciated. Don't forget a full-length mirror.

FINGER FOOD BUFFET

The menu for 40

Assorted savouries on sticks (for
hot kebabs, see page 33)
Anchovy fingers
Ham cornets

Tiny hamburgers
Toasted cheese whirls
Savoury stuffed rolls
Pineapple or melon dip

The recipes

ASSORTED SAVOURIES ON STICKS

(1) Wrap anchovy fillets round cocktail onions. (2) Remove stones from cooked prunes and fill with seasoned cream cheese. (3) Wrap tiny thin rashers of bacon round stuffed olives. (4) Put together firm cubes of cheese and cocktail onions. Put all these on sticks in small sweet cases. You will need 160.

ANCHOVY FINGERS

Soak some fillets of anchovy in a little milk to remove excess salt. Roll out some puff pastry very thinly then cut into fingers roughly the size of the fillets. Twist an anchovy fillet and a finger of pastry together, pinch both ends, place on a baking sheet, brush with beaten egg and bake at Gas Reg. No. 5 (379 deg. F.) for 12 to 15 mins. You will need 180 to 240 of these.

HAM CORNETS

Using cream horn tins, make cornets of thinly rolled puff pastry. Brush with beaten egg and bake at Gas Reg. No. 6 (403 deg. F.) for 15 mins. Fill with minced ham bound with a little mayonnaise and chutney. You will need 120 of these.

TINY HAMBURGERS

INGREDIENTS: 6lbs lean steak, minced; 6 level teaspoonsful salt; 2 level teaspoonsful pepper; 6 tablespoonsful grated onion; 6 eggs; butter for frying.

METHOD: Mix the minced steak with the seasoning, onion and beaten eggs. Shape into very small rounds and fry for about 6 mins on each side in the hot butter. These can be served on halves of florin-sized bridge rolls. Get your baker to make you some bridge roll dough into little florin-sized buns.

TOASTED CHEESE WHIRLS

Make roly-poly sandwiches (see page 89) filled with tangy cheese spread —grated cheese mixed with a little English mustard and a drop of vinegar. Cut these into slices, dip into beaten egg and then into grated cheese and bake until gold and crisp. You will need 120 to 180 of these (cut from 20 to 30 rolls).

SAVOURY ROLLS

Fill tiny florin-sized rolls (get your baker to make these for you) with minced chicken, minced ham or any savoury mixture. You will need 120 of these.

PINEAPPLE OR MELON DIP

(See page 31 for Fruit and Cheese Dip).

THE 2A.M. BREAKFAST

The menu for 40

Fried eggs and bacon
Pork sausages
Scrambled eggs
Sauté kidneys
Mushrooms

Lager or light ale
Coffee
Rolls or French bread and butter
Hot soup on departure

Quantities for 40 persons

FRIED EGGS AND BACON: *6lbs best back rashers; 7 doz eggs*
PORK SAUSAGES: *7lbs large pork sausages (8 to the pound)*

SCRAMBLED EGGS: *4 doz eggs*
SAUTÉ KIDNEYS: *6lbs veal kidney or 20 lambs' kidneys*
MUSHROOMS: *2lbs of mushrooms*

The drinks

Calculate as follows:
Sherry (10 drinks from 1 bottle)
Gin (14 drinks from 1 bottle)
Whisky (14 drinks from 1 bottle)
Sparkling French, German or Italian wine (6 glasses per bottle)
Rosé, white wine or champagne (6 glasses per bottle)

Pimmletts (1 bottle of Pimms and 8 bottles of lemonade serve 30 drinks in 8oz goblets)
2 to 3 gallons fruit cup
Lager: 4 doz bottles or 30 pts light ale
Coffee: 1 gallon black; 4pts milk
Soup: 10pts

Equipment for 40

2 or 3 doz coffee cups and saucers
and spoons (4 doz if you do not
have adequate kitchen help)
6 large spoons and forks for serving the hot food
6 doz paper napkins
2 or 3 large jugs for hot milk
2 or 3 sugar basins
2 or 3 baskets for rolls or hot
French bread
3 large glass jugs for fruit cup
40 soup cups (tea cups may
be used)
1 cwt block of ice for drinks (order
this from your fishmonger)

80 Paris goblets (8 oz)
2 doz sherry glasses
2 trays for handing drinks
Several ashtrays
Attractive plates and trays for
finger food
3 doz lager or Worthington glasses
Up to 6 large platters for breakfast food
60 medium-sized meat plates
2 or 3 doz knives and forks
2 or 3 doz butter knives (these can
be washed in between if you have
good kitchen help, otherwise
4 doz)

INDEX

First published 1963 by Pitkin Pictorials Ltd

This edition published 2007 by Macmillan
an imprint of Pan Macmillan Ltd
Pan Macmillan, 20 New Wharf Road, London N1 9RR
Basingstoke and Oxford
Associated companies throughout the world
www.panmacmillan.com

ISBN 978-0-230-70101-4

Copyright © The Telegraph Group 1963 and 2007

The right of Evelyn Payne to be identified as the
author of this work has been asserted by her in accordance
with the Copyright, Designs and Patents Act 1988.

1 3 5 7 9 8 6 4 2

A CIP catalogue record for this book is available from
the British Library.

Printed and bound in Great Britain by
Mackays of Chatham plc, Chatham, Kent

Visit **www.panmacmillan.com** to read more about all our books
and to buy them. You will also find features, author interviews and
news of any author events, and you can sign up for e-newsletters
so that you're always first to hear about our new releases.